NEPALI
phrasebook

Mary-Jo O'Rourke

Bimal Shrestha

Nepali phrasebook
 3rd edition

Published by
 Lonely Planet Publications
 Head Office: PO Box 617, Hawthorn, Vic 3122, Australia
 Branches: 155 Filbert St, Suite 251, Oakland, CA 94607, USA
            10 Barley Mow Passage, Chiswick, W4 4PH, UK
            71 bis rue du Cardinal Lemoine, 75005 Paris, France

Printed by
 Colorcraft Ltd, Hong Kong

Cover Photograph
 Face of Sweta Bhairab in Durbar Square, Kathmandu, Nepal
 (Richard Everist)

Published
 October 1996

National Library of Australia Cataloguing in Publication Data

O'Rourke, Mary Jo.
 Nepali phrasebook.

 3rd ed.
 Includes index.
 ISBN 0 86442 345 4.

 1. Nepali language - Conversation and phrase-books - English. I. Shrestha,
 Bimal. II. Title. (Series: Lonely Planet language survival kit).

491.49

Contents

Introduction...7

Abbreviations Used in This
  Book.....................................9

Getting Started........................ 9

Pronunciation 11

Vowels 11
Consonants 12

Word Stress 14

Grammar...16

Word Order.............................16
Nouns 17
Demonstratives.......................17
Adjectives 18
Pronouns 18
Verbs 22
To Be 27

Possession...............................32
Imperative 32
Necessity 32
Questions 33
Postpositions...........................34
Conjunctions 35
'Other' 36

Greetings & Civilities 37

Greetings 37
Please & Thank You 38
Hajur......................................38
Attracting Someone's
  Attention....................................38

Some Useful Phrases 39
Body Language &
  Etiquette............................ 40
Tips & Gift-Giving 41
Common Expressions............ 42

Small Talk 43

Top 10 Useful Phrases 43
Yes & No.................................44
Language Difficulties 44
Meeting People.......................46
Nationalities............................47
Age 49
Occupations.............................49
Religion....................................51

Family 51
Feelings 54
Opinions.................................. 56
Making Conversation 56
Interests 57
Special Occasions 58
Interjections............................. 59
Some Useful Phrases 59

Getting Around 61

Finding Your Way	61	Bicycle Hire	65
Directions	62	Bus	65
Transport	63	Taxi & Rickshaw	66
Buying Tickets	64	Some Useful Words	68

Accommodation 69

Finding Accommodation	70	Some Useful Phrases	76
At the Hotel	70	Some Useful Words	77

Around Town 79

At the Embassy	79	At the Bank	82
At the Post Office	80	Sightseeing	83
Telephone	81	Some Useful Words	85

Trekking 87

Hiring Porters	88	Birds	97
Asking Directions	89	Insects	98
Along the Way	91	Plants	99
Weather	93	Some Useful Phrases	99
Geographical Terms	95	Some Useful Words	101
Animals	96		

Food 102

At the Restaurant	104	Some Useful Phrases	113
At the Market	106	Some Useful Words	113
Drinks	112		

Shopping 115

Bargaining	117	Photography	123
Souvenirs	118	Smoking	123
Clothing	119	Weights & Measures	124
Colours	121	Size & Quantity	124
Toiletries	122	Some Useful Phrases	125
Stationery & Publications	122	Some Useful Words	127

Health 129

Complaints	130	Parts of the Body	134
Women's Health	133	At the Chemist	136
Allergies	133	Some Useful Phrases	136
The Doctor Might Say	133	Some Useful Words	137

Time, Dates & Festivals 139

Telling the Time 139
Days of the Week 140
The Nepali Calendar 140
Present 141
Past 142

Future 142
Some Useful Words 142
Some Useful Phrases 143
Festivals 144
Gods & Prominent Beings ... 147

Numbers & Amounts 156

Cardinal Numbers 156
Ordinal Numbers 157

Counters 157
Fractions 158

Vocabulary 159

Emergencies 199

Index 202

From the Publisher
This edition was edited by Lou Callan and proofread by Sally Steward. Penelope Richardson and Bishnu Shrestha provided the illustrations, and layout of the book was by Stella Vassiliou. David Kemp designed the cover.

About the Authors
This edition was written by Mary-Jo O'Rourke and Bimal Man Shrestha.

Mary-Jo O'Rourke is a linguist, writer and editor with a long-held interest in Nepal and its people. She is currently doing an MA in Newari.

Bimal Man Shrestha resides in both Kathmandu and Melbourne. He is bilingual in Newari and Nepali and speaks several other languages fluently. He has worked as a tourist guide and as an interpreter and translator in various languages.

Acknowledgements
The authors wish to thank family and friends around the world for their support and encouragement. Lively discussion of cross-cultural communication in Nepal has been helpful (usually) and entertaining (always)!

Thanks also to Dan Levin for his assistance with fonts and script.

Introduction

Nepal became very popular with travellers from all over the world when it opened its long-closed doors to foreigners in 1951. Most Nepalis you are likely to meet will speak some English, especially in urban and popular tourist areas. However, as a traveller you'll find that life in a foreign country is a lot easier and more interesting if you try to learn a little of the language. Even if you're not fluent, being able to communicate on a basic level will help to narrow the cultural gap and so deepen your experience of a different society.

Trekking is one of the most popular activities for travellers in Nepal, and if you want to move away from the main tourist centres it can be difficult to find local people who speak more than rudimentary English, as many hill villages still lack even the most basic educational facilities.

Nepali belongs to the Indo-European language family, and so is closely related to Hindi, and distantly related to English, French and German. Nepali is not only the national language of Nepal, it is also widely spoken in Sikkim, Darjeeling and other parts of

7

India, Tibet and Bhutan. Altogether it is spoken by some 30 million people. Peace Corps volunteers and other long-term foreign residents of Nepal are among the many non-native speakers of Nepali, and it is also a second language for about 50% of the population. In this ethnically heterogenous country of 19 million people and more than 30 indigenous languages, Nepali, as the national language, provides a lingua franca for the many different ethnic groups, and acts as a unifying force among its diverse people.

Nepali has a number of dialects, or different accents. This phrasebook uses the standard form, which is understood throughout most of the country. Nepali is written in the Devanagari script, a writing form also used for Hindi, and for Sanskrit which is the parent of both languages. As in English, the alphabet is written left-to-right. Most consonants are written below a horizontal line, which is what gives Devanagari its distinctive look, while vowels may occur beside, above or below the consonants.

There are some significant differences between everyday spoken Nepali and the more formal written language. However, the information in this book is presented in the informal spoken style which is all that travellers will find necessary. Nepali is a fairly easy language to learn, and this phrasebook concentrates on conversational Nepali, not the finer points of grammar. Nepali has a smaller vocabulary than English, which means that a Nepali word often has a much more general meaning than in English, and so may have several translations. For instance, *raamro* means 'good' but can also mean 'nice' or 'beautiful'.

This phrasebook now includes the Devanagari script as well as the phonetic transcription in Roman script. If you're having trouble making yourself understood, just point to the script on the right-hand side of the page. All you need to make learning Nepali enjoyable are a few Nepali companions to practise with, and that will prove impossible to avoid in friendly Nepal. So, gather a few phrases from this book, and prepare yourself for some fascinating encounters.

Good luck in your travels and *namaste!*

Abbreviations Used in This Book

adj	adjective	n	noun
f	feminine	pl	plural
inf	informal	sg	singular
m	masculine	v	verb

Getting Started

There are a few useful words you should try memorising before your trip. The word *namaste* (pronounced *na-ma-stay*), can be used to mean both 'Hello' and 'Goodbye' (and 'Good luck'!). 'Please' and 'Thankyou' are used less frequently than in English (see Greetings & Civilities, page 38), but it's a good idea to remember *hajur (ha-joor)*, which is used in many contexts: as a query like 'Excuse me?' or 'Pardon?' if you don't understand something; as a general politeness when you say 'Yes', *ho hajur*, and 'No', *hoina hajur*, and just as a way of expressing agreement.

You'll need to remember *kati ho?*, 'How much is it?', while other essentials include *kahā̃? (ka-haang)*, 'Where?', and *kahile*, 'When?'. 'I didn't understand' is *maile bujhina* (pronounced *ma-ee-lay booj-hee-na)*. 'Do you speak English?' is a tricky one, so remember that it's on page 44, where you can point to the Nepali script.

Pronunciation

Nepali is fairly easy to pronounce. There are no tones, such as in Thai. Many of the vowel and consonant sounds of English are also found in Nepali. There are a few consonants with no English equivalent, but these are not difficult to learn. The Nepali alphabet has 67 characters and, unlike English, most of them have only one pronunciation. Likewise, most Nepali sounds have only one spelling. This almost one-to-one correspondence between sounds and letters means that spelling in Nepali is much more straightforward than in English. Every letter contains part of (or is written relative to) a horizontal line, and letters are joined together into words by this line.

Vowels

There are six vowels and two vowel combinations (diphthongs) in Nepali. Most of these also occur as nasal vowels, making 15 vowels in all. The nasals are similar to those of French, with the airstream coming out of the nose, and are indicated in the text by a tilde (~) over the vowel or sometimes by a nasal consonant ('n' or 'm') following it. Long vowels are indicated by a line (macron) over the vowel.

11

Vowels have two forms: a full one when written alone or at the beginning of a word or syllable, and another abbreviated one when written after a consonant. Vowels may be written above, below or beside consonants, and even in front.

a/ā	short sound like the 'u' in 'hut', except after 'p', 'b' and 'm' when it is more like the 'o' in 'not'
ā/ā̃	long sound, as the 'a' in 'garden'
e/ẽ	short sound, as the 'é' in the French word *soufflé* or the 'ay' in 'may'
i/ī	always pronounced as the 'ee' in 'seem'
o	as the 'o' in 'ox'
u/ū	as the 'oo' in 'boot'
ai/aĩ	a diphthong, as the 'i' in 'mine'
au/aũ	as the 'ow' in 'now' but shorter

short vowels: *a, ā, i, u, ū*
long vowels: *ā, ā̃, e, ẽ, ai, aĩ, o, au, aũ*

Consonants

Most of the consonants are pronounced as in English with the exception of the following. When Nepali consonants are doubled they must be pronounced with their full double force.

y	as the 'y' in 'yes' but shorter
r	always trilled slightly, and clearer than the English 'r'
l	as in English but always clear
sh	as the 'sh' in 'short' (many speakers pronounce it as the English 's')
h	more forcefully than in English, except in the middle of a word, where it is hardly pronounced at all.

Aspirated Consonants

Aspiration is an important part of Nepali pronunciation. The aspirated consonants are pronounced more forcefully than their unaspirated counterparts. Pronounce them with a strong puff of air, like the 'th' in 'hothouse'. English does have both types of consonants but, unlike Nepali, doesn't use them to differentiate between words. Aspiration is indicated in the text by the letter 'h' following the consonant, so 'th' represents an aspirated 't'. Don't confuse this with the English sound 'th', as in 'think' or 'then', which does not occur at all in Nepali. The aspirated 'ph' is generally pronounced as in 'haphazard' although you may come across it sounding like an 'f'. The consonant 'c' is pronounced as 'ch' in 'chair' but with less breathiness, while 'ch' is more breathy. The 'j' sound is normally pronounced as 'j' in 'join' but may also be pronounced as 'ds' in 'bands' or as 'z' in 'zoo'.

Retroflex Consonants

Retroflex sounds are made by curling your tongue up and back towards the roof of your mouth. In Nepali the 't' and 'd' sounds, both ordinary and aspirated, also occur as retroflex sounds. These are the sounds that make the Indian and Nepali pronunciation of English so distinctive. They are not too difficult to get the hang of with a bit of practice. Try saying the sound several times, moving your tongue a bit further back along the roof of your mouth each time.

Retroflex 'd' and 'dh' are sometimes also pronounced as a retroflex 'r', which is a quick flap of the tongue against the roof of the mouth, like the 'd' sound in 'ladder' when said quickly. Retroflex consonants are indicated throughout the text by **bold** type.

Word Stress

The position of the stressed syllable in Nepali words depends on the vowel length, and on whether the syllables are open (end in vowels) or closed (end in consonants). As a rough guide, in words of two syllables the last syllable is normally the stressed one, while in words of three or more syllables the second-last syllable is stressed. Stress is indicated here by an underline.

In words of two syllables, if the last syllable is closed and contains a long vowel, then it is stressed. Otherwise the first syllable is stressed:

cigarette	*chu-<u>rot</u>*
from now	*<u>a</u>-ba*

In words of more than two syllables, there are three possible stress patterns. They are listed here in order of frequency:

1. If the second-last syllable has a long vowel, then it is stressed:

border	*si-<u>mā</u>-ā*

2. If the final syllable is closed, with two final consonants or a long vowel, then it is stressed:

India	*hin-du-<u>stān</u>*

3. If the second-last syllable is short and the last syllable is open, or closed with a short vowel and one consonant, then the third-last syllable is stressed:

lightweight <u>ha</u>-lu-ko

Grammar

This section contains some basic information about the structure of Nepali, and a few general grammar rules. It will enable you to learn the language quickly to a point where you can communicate simply, by using the vocabulary in this book with the basic sentence patterns provided.

Word Order

The verb usually comes at the end of a sentence, so that the word order is generally subject-object-verb.

One of the distinguishing features of spoken Nepali is that it is often used in a kind of shorthand way, when compared with written usage. Information that is clear from the context, or not relevant in a particular situation, will often be left out. This often includes subject pronouns, particularly the first person singular ('I'). Spoken Nepali is also sometimes grammatically simplified. For example, singular forms are often used with a plural meaning.

My name is Anita.   *mero nām anita ho*
                                   (lit: my name Anita is)

16

This is my friend.   *yo mero sāthi ho*
                                 (lit: this my friend is)

Nouns

Nouns in Nepali are single words, and there are no articles like the English 'the' or 'a'. To make a noun plural, add the ending *-haru*, although this is often left out in speech when plurality is clear from the context, or not important. Nouns (and pronouns) can have different endings depending on how they are used in the sentence. (See Pronouns, page 18.)

a friend	*sāthi*
friends	*sāthi-haru*

Demonstratives

As Nepali has no articles, the demonstrative adjectives – 'this' and 'that' – are in common use, both in front of nouns and alone.

this	*yo*	these	*yi*
that	*tyo*	those	*ti*

this girl	*yo keti*	these girls	*yi keti-haru*
that girl	*tyo keti*	those girls	*ti keti-haru*

Note that, in informal speech, singular forms are often used with plural subjects:

those people   *ti/tyo mānche-haru*

GRAMMAR

Adjectives

As in English, Nepali adjectives precede the nouns they refer to:

an expensive shop   *mahango pasal*

To compare anything, use -*bhandā* ('than') or *sab-bhandā* ('than all'):

Ram is fatter than Anita.
  rām anita-bhandā moto cha
  (lit: Ram Anita-than fat is)
Kathmandu is Nepal's largest city.
  kāthmādaũ nepāl-ko sab-bhandā thulo shahar ho
  (lit: Kathmandu Nepal-**possessive** than-all large city is)

Pronouns

Pronouns have both formal and informal variations. You should use the formal ones, except with intimate friends, children and animals. Unless indicated otherwise, the formal, more polite variation is used in this book.

Pronouns (and nouns) have different endings according to their use in a sentence (as subject, object or possessive, etc). These endings translate as prepositions like 'to', 'of' and 'with' in English.

Like nouns, pronouns have no gender. There are three third person singular pronouns and each of them can mean 'he', 'she' or 'it', except *u* which can only mean 'he' or 'she'. Pronouns are often omitted in speech when they can be understood from the context, for example, when they are the subject of the sentence.

Subject Pronouns

I	*ma*
we	*hāmi(haru)*
you (sg, inf)	*timi*
you (pl, inf)	*timiharu*
you (sg)	*tapāĩ*
you (pl)	*tapāĩharu*
he/she/it (inf)	*u/tyo/yo*
they (inf)	*uniharu*
he/she/it	*wahā̃*
they	*wahā̃haru*

Note that for 'we', the short form *hāmi* is often used instead of the full form *hāmiharu*. Remember also that *u* and *uniharu* are used only for people, not things.

Subject pronouns are used without any additional endings in simple sentences that contain no objects.

I go	*ma jānchu*
he/she (inf) does	*u garcha*

Subject pronouns of sentences with objects take the ending *-le*. There are some irregular forms, however: the first person singular *(maile)* and the third person singular *(usle, tyasle, yasle)*. This ending makes no difference to the meaning, and translates as an ordinary subject – *maile bujhchu* means 'I understand (it)'.

GRAMMAR

The ending *-le* can also be attached to nouns, and translates as 'by, with, from, of, in', according to the context.

> in the opinion of the government
> *sarkār-ko rāya-le*
> (lit: government-**possessive** opinion-*le*)

Object Pronouns

In Nepali object nouns and pronouns (both direct and indirect) normally take the ending *-lāi*, particularly if the object is a name or refers to a person. The ending *-lāi* often translates as 'to' or 'for':

I give it to you.　　　　　*ma tapāĩ-lāi dinchu*
　　　　　　　　　　　　(lit: I you-to give)

If the object is not human, *-lāi* is usually left out:

He/She is feeding the dog.　*u kukur khuwāũ-dai-cha*
　　　　　　　　　　　　(lit: he/she dog is-feeding)

Possessive Pronouns

The possessive ending for both nouns and pronouns is *-ko* but some possessive pronouns are irregular, and so they are all listed below:

my	*mero*
our	*hāmro*
your (sg, inf)	*timro*
your (pl, inf)	*timiharuko*
your (sg)	*tapāīko*
your (pl)	*tapāīharuko*
his/her/its (inf)	*usko/tyasko/yasko*
his/her/its	*wahāko*
their (inf)	*uniharuko*
their	*wahāharuko*

This is our dog. *yo hāmro kukur ho*
(lit: this our dog is)

The possessive pronouns may also stand alone, in which case they translate as 'mine, ours, yours, his, hers, its, theirs'.

Is this yours? *yo tapāī-ko ho?*
(lit: this yours is?)

As in English, possessives come before the nouns they refer to:

my cat *mero birālo*
Ram's shirt *rām-ko kamij*
(lit: Ram-**possessive** shirt)

Verbs

Verb formation in Nepali is fairly straightforward, except with the verb 'to be' (see page 27). There are many tenses, but you really only need to know the present and past tense forms, in both affirmative and negative. Simple additions to these basic tenses give you the continuous, future and imperative (orders/requests) verb forms. Don't be put off by the verb lists, they are there to make it easy for you to look up the verb form you need.

Nepali verbs are made up of two parts: the stem and the tense ending. The stem stays the same. The ending changes according to the person (first, second, third) and plurality of the subject pronoun. Infinitives (the dictionary form) end in *-nu*:

to do	*garnu*
to eat	*khānu*
to go	*jānu*

Present Tense

I do	*ma gar-chu*
you (sg, inf) do	*timi gar-chau*
he/she/it (inf) does	*u/tyo/yo gar-cha*
we do	*hāmi gar-chaũ*
you (sg, inf) do	*timiharu gar-chau*
they (inf) do	*uniharu gar-cha*

The present tense verb forms corresponding to the formal pronouns all take the same ending, *huncha*:

you (sg/pl) do	*tapāĩ(haru) garnu huncha*
he/she/it does	*wahā̃ garnu huncha*
they do	*wahā̃haru garnu huncha*

Verbs whose stems end in a vowel keep the *n*:

to go	*jā-nu*	I go	*ma jān-chu*
to come	*āu-nu*	I come	*ma āun-chu*

The present tense is used for regular or habitual actions, and corresponds to the present tense in English:

I work every day.   *ma dinhū kām garchu*
                    (lit: I daily work do)

As in English, it can also be used to indicate the future:

Next week we go to Nepal.   *āune haptā hāmi nepal*
                            janchaŭ
                            (lit: next week we Nepal go)

Negation

There is no single negative form in Nepali that corresponds to 'not' in English. Instead, the verb forms for each subject change in the negative, but they follow a pattern and are not difficult to learn. Positive and negative forms are listed together in all verb sections. The present tense negatives are given here.

I do not go	*ma jān-dina*
we do not go	*hāmi jān-dainaū*
you (inf) do not go	*timi(haru) jān-dainau*
he/she/it (inf) does not go	*u/tyo/yo ā jān-daina*
they (inf) do not go	*uniharu jān-dainan*

To negate polite forms, add *-hunna* to the infinitive:

you (sg) do not go	*tapāī jānu-hunna*
you (pl) do not go	*tapāīharu jānu-hunna*
he/she/it does not go	*wahā̃ jānu-hunna*
they do not go	*wahā̃haru jānu-hunna*

Continuous Tense

This tense is formed by inserting *-dai-* between the verb stem and the ending. Present, past and future tenses can also be continuous, meaning that the action goes on for a period of time. The present continuous is the most common tense in spoken Nepali, and corresponds to the English present continuous. Like the simple present, it may also be used for the future.

I am eating	*ma khān-dai-chu*
you (sg) are eating	*timi khān-dai-chau*
he/she/it (inf) is eating	*u/tyo/yo khān-dai-cha*
we are eating	*hāmi khān-dai-chaū*
you (pl) are eating	*timiharu khān-dai-chau*
they (inf) are eating	*uniharu khān-dai-chan*

The formal variations are as follows:

you (sg) are eating	*tapāī khān-dai-hunu huncha*
you (pl) are eating	*tapāīharu khān-dai-hunu huncha*
he/she/it is eating	*wahā̃ khān-dai-hunu huncha*
they are eating	*wahā̃haru khān-dai-hunu huncha*

Past Tense

The past is used for completed actions, and corresponds to the English past tense. When the sentence has an object, the subject in the past always takes the ending *-le:*

I did	*mai(-le) garẽ*
I didn't	*mai(-le) garinā*
you (sg, inf) did	*timi(-le) garyau*
you (sg, inf) didn't	*timi(-le) garenau*
he/she/it (inf) did	*us(-le)/tyas(-le)/yas(-le) garyo*
he/she/it (inf) didn't	*us(-le)/tyas(-le)/yas(-le) garena*
we did	*hāmi(-le) garyaū*
we didn't	*hāmi(-le) garenaū*
you (pl, inf) did	*timiharu(-le) garyau*
you (pl, inf) didn't	*timiharu(-le) garenau*
they (inf) did	*uniharu(-le) gare*
they (inf) didn't	*uniharu(-le) garenan*

The formal variations add *-bhayo* and *-bhaena* to the infinitive:

you (sg) did	*tapāī(-le) garnu bhayo*
you (sg) didn't	*tapāī(-le) garnu bhaena*
He/She did not speak.	*wahā̃(-le) bolnu bhaena*

Verbs whose stems end in a vowel, drop the final vowel in the past tense:

to come	*āunu*
I come	*ma āun-chu*
I came	*ma ā-ē*

Future Tense

The most common future tense used in spoken Nepali is formed by using the verb in the present tense followed by the third person singular future form of 'to be' – *holā*.

I will go.	*ma jānchu holā*
	(lit: I go will-be)
He/She will not go.	*u jāndaina holā*
	(lit: he/she not-go will-be)

The Neutral Infinitive

In conversation, Nepalis commonly use a versatile neutral verb form for present and, especially, future tenses. It is used mainly in short statements and questions, and pronouns are usually left out. This is the simplest verb form to use when you get stuck!

The ending *-ne* replaces the infinitive ending *-nu* to form this neutral verb. Its negative is formed simply with the prefix *na-*:

What will we do today?	*āja ke garne?*
	(lit: today what to-do?)

Let's go out.	*bāhira jāne*
	(lit: outside to-go)
Let's not go out.	*bāhira najāne*
	(lit: outside not-to-go)

To Be

The Nepali verb 'to be' *(hunu)* is complex, and full detail is given below to make it easy to refer back to. There are three alternate versions: *cha*, *ho* and *huncha*, each used in different ways.

Cha and *ho* are the most common. They both mean 'is' but *cha* is used for locating, that is, indicating where, and *ho* is used for defining, that is, indicating 'who, how, what'.

Present

cha	
I am	*ma chu*
I am not	*ma chaina*
you (sg, inf) are	*timi chau*
you (sg, inf) are not	*timi chainau*
he/she/it (inf) is	*u/tyo/yo cha*
he/she/it (inf) is not	*u/tyo/yo chaina*
we are	*hāmi chāu*
we are not	*hāmi chaināu*
you (pl, inf) are	*timiharu chau*
you (pl, inf) are not	*timiharu chainau*
they (inf) are	*uniharu chan*
they (inf) are not	*uniharu chainan*

GRAMMAR

ho	
I am	*ma hũ*
I am not	*ma hoina*
you (sg, inf) are	*timi hau*
you (sg, inf) are not	*timi hoinau*
he/she/it (inf) is	*u/tyo/yo ho*
he/she/it (inf) is not	*u/tyo/yo hoina*
we are	*hāmi haũ*
we are not	*hāmi hoinaũ*
you (pl, inf) are	*timiharu hau*
you (pl, inf) are not	*timiharu hoinau*
they are	*uniharu hun*
they are not	*uniharu hoinan*

My house is in Nepal.   *mero ghar nepāl-mā cha*
(lit: my house Nepal-in is)

My mother is a doctor.   *mero āmā dāktar ho*
(lit: my mother doctor is)

huncha	
I am	*ma hunchu*
I am not	*ma hundina*
you (sg, inf) are	*timi hunchau*
you (sg, inf) are not	*timi hundainau*
he/she/it is	*u/tyo/yo huncha*
he/she/it is not	*u/tyo/yo hundaina*
we are	*hāmi hunchaū*
we are not	*hāmi hundainaū*
you (pl, inf) are	*timiharu hunchau*
you (pl, inf) are not	*timiharu hundainau*
they (inf) are	*uniharu hunchan*
they (inf) are not	*uniharu hundainan*

The formal versions are the same for *cha, ho* and *huncha:*

you (sg/pl) are	*tapāī(haru) hunu huncha*
you (sg/pl) are not	*tapāī(haru) hunu hunna*
he/she/it is	*wahā̃ hunu huncha*
he/she/it is not	*wahā̃ hunu hunna*
they are	*wahā̃haru hunu huncha*
they are not	*wahā̃haru hunu hunna*

Huncha also translates as 'is' but, unlike *cha* or *ho, huncha* refers to general facts or events:

This mango is sweet.	*yo āmp guliyo cha/ho* (lit: this mango sweet is)
Mangos are sweet.	*āmp guliyo huncha* (lit: mango sweet is)

Past

cha & ho	
I was	*ma thiẽ*
I was not	*ma thiinā*
you (sg, inf) were	*timi thiyau*
you (sg, inf) were not	*timi thienau*
he/she/it (inf) was	*u/tyo/yo thiyo*
he/she/it (inf) was not	*u/tyo/yo thiena*
we were	*hāmi thiyaũ*
we were not	*hāmi thienaũ*
you (pl, inf) were	*timiharu thiyau*
you (pl, inf) were not	*timiharu thienau*
they were	*uniharu thie*
they were not	*uniharu thienan*

The formal variations are as follows:

you (sg/pl) were	*tapāĩ(haru) hunu hunthyo*
you (sg/pl) were not	*tapāĩ(haru) hunu hunnathyo*
he/she/it was	*wahā̃ hunu hunthyo*
he/she/it was not	*wahā̃ hunu hunnathyo*
they were	*wahā̃haru hunu hunthyo*
they were not	*wahā̃haru hunu hunnathyo*

huncha	
I was	*ma bhaẽ*
I was not	*ma bhainã*
you (sg, inf) were	*timi bhayau*
you (sg, inf) were not	*timi bhaenau*
he/she/it was	*u/tyo/yo bhayo*
he/she/it was not	*u/tyo/yo bhaena*
we were	*hāmi bhayaũ*
we were not	*hāmi bhaenaũ*
you (pl, inf) were	*timiharu bhayau*
you (pl, inf) were not	*timiharu bhaenau*
they were	*uniharu bhae*
they were not	*uniharu bhaenan*

The formal variations are as follows:

you (sg/pl) were	*tapāī(haru) hunu bhayo*
you (sg/pl) were not	*tapāī(haru) hunu bhaena*
he/she/it was	*wahā̃ hunu bhayo*
he/she/it was not	*wahā̃ hunu bhaena*
they were	*wahā̃haru hunu bhayo*
they were not	*wahā̃haru hunu bhaena*

The verb *bhayo* is often pronounced just *ho*, especially when used as a common interjection meaning 'Enough/Stop'. It may also mean 'happened' or 'became' in some idioms:

What's the matter?	*ke bhayo/bho?*
	(lit: what happened?)
It has become hot.	*garmi bhayo*
	(lit: hot became)

Possession

In Nepali there is no verb equivalent to the English 'to have', but the idea of possession may be expressed using a form of *cha* plus a possessive noun or pronoun:

> He/She has five children.   *usko pānc janā chorā-chori chan*
> (lit: he/she five people children have)

If the possession is portable, the postposition (see page 34) meaning 'with', *-sanga* or *-sita*, is added to the possessor:

> I don't have a pen.   *ma-sanga kalam chaina*
> (lit: I-with pen am-not)

Imperative

This verb form is used for giving orders or making requests. To make a polite imperative, add the suffix *-hos* to the infinitive ending *-nu*. To make this negative, use the prefix *na-*:

> Please eat.   *khānu-hos*
> (lit: to-eat-**imperative**)
> Please don't tell me.   *ma-lāi na-bhannu-hos*
> (lit: I-to **negative**-tell-**imperative**)

Necessity

To express necessity, use the infinitive of a verb plus a third person singular form of the common verb *parnu* ('to be necessary'). The subject is usually omitted. If the subject is expressed it takes the ending *-le* when the sentence contains an object and *-lāi* when there is no object.

> It is necessary to walk there.
>   *tyahā̃ hĩdnu-parcha*
>   (lit: there walk-must)
> It isn't necessary to come to this office.
>   *yo kāryālaya-mā āunu-parcha*
>   (lit: this office-to come-must-not)
> I have to wash these clothes.
>   *maile yo lugā dhunu-parcha*
>   (lit: I-*le* this clothing wash-must)

GRAMMAR

Questions

In Nepali the simplest way to ask a question is to raise the intonation of your voice at the end of the sentence. Answer this type of question by repeating the main verb in the affirmative or negative:

Are you Nepali?	*tapāī nepāli hunu huncha?*
	(lit: you Nepali are?)
Yes.	*hunu huncha*
No.	*hunu hunna*

You can also use interrogative words, which normally come just before the verb in the sentence, and include the following:

how (means)	*kasari*
how (quality)	*kasto*
how much/many	*kati*
where	*kahā̃*
what	*ke*
when	*kahile*
why	*kina*
who	*ko*
whose	*kasko*
which	*kun*
anyone	*kohi*
anything	*kehi*

Where is the tiger?	*bāgh kahā̃ cha?*
	(lit: tiger where is?)
Whose book is this?	*yo kitāb kasko ho?*
	(lit: this book whose is?)
Is anyone there?	*kohi hunu huncha?*

Postpositions

These words indicate relative location and direction. What we call 'prepositions' in English, come after the noun in Nepali and so are called postpositions. They can be used with adverbs and personal pronouns.

about	-tira
after	-pachi
at/in/on/to (place)	-mā
behind	-pachādi
between	-bic
by/with	-le
far	-tādhā
for (the sake of)	-kolāgi
from (time)	-dekhi
from (place)	-bāta
in front of	-agādi
in(side)	-bhitra
near/close	-najik
of	-ko
out(side)	-bāhira
to (person, animal)	-lāi
under	-muni
up	-māthi
with/by	-sanga/sita
without	-bina

GRAMMAR

Conjunctions

and	ra
because	kinabhane
but	tara
or	ki
otherwise	natra
then	ani

'Other'

There are two words in Nepali meaning 'other': *arko* ('the other of two'), is used mainly with singular nouns, while *aru* ('other/ else'), is used with plural nouns and things that can't be counted:

> I'll give you the other book.
>> *tapāī-lāi arko kitāb dinchu*
>> (lit: you-to other book I-give)
>
> Drink some more tea.
>> *aru ciyā khānu-hos*
>> (lit: more tea drink-**imperative**)

Greetings & Civilities

The Nepalis are very friendly people and love to chat *(gaph garnu)* – you could call it a national pastime. So you won't find any barriers to conversation, which will probably proceed in a mixture of Nepali and English. English is compulsory in Nepali schools, and many people will be eager to practise it with you, especially in urban and popular tourist areas.

However, the use of even a few Nepali phrases will add to your understanding and enjoyment of Nepal, and ensure your share of warm Nepali hospitality is even warmer!

Greetings

The first thing you need to know is the general Nepali greeting, *namaste*. This expression can mean 'Hello' and 'Goodbye'. *Namaste* literally means 'I bow to the god in you'. *Namaskār* is an even more polite form of the same greeting, but less commonly used in Nepal. Both should be accompanied by the gesture of palms held together in front of the face, as if in prayer.

Hello/Goodbye.	*namaste/namaskār*	नमस्ते / नमस्कार
How are you?	*tapāīlāi kasto cha?*	तपाईंलाई कस्तो छ ?
(formal)	*ārāmai hunu huncha?*	आरामै हुनुहुन्छ ?
I'm fine.	*malāi sancai cha*	मलाई सन्चै छ
And you?	*ani tapāīlāi?*	अनि तपाईंलाई ?
Goodnight.	*subha rātri*	सुभरात्रि

Please & Thank You

The Nepali word for 'Please' *(kripayā)* is very formal and is reserved mainly for writing. Spoken Nepali uses the imperative verb suffix *-hos* (see Grammar, page 32). Similarly, the word for 'Thank you' *(dhanyabād)* is not used as commonly as the English word. It would be inappropriate to use *dhanyabād* in shops or restaurants. *Dhanyabād* is best kept to express thanks for particular favours.

'Hajur'

This is a handy word, which can be used in several different ways. Literally, it means 'Sir', but this is not how it is used. *Hajur* may be used for both sexes. If someone calls out to you, the correct response is *Hajur?* It is also used to express agreement or confirm what someone has just said to you. *Hajur* may be added to the answer of a simple 'Yes/No' question, for the sake of politeness. If you did not hear or understand something said to you, and want it repeated, you need simply say *Hajur?*

Attracting Someone's Attention

To attract someone's attention, call *o*, plus one of the kinship terms (see Small Talk, page 52). You then say *namaste* and make your request. To beckon someone from a distance, wave your hand toward yourself, with palm facing down and fingers also pointing downwards. There is a special form of address for the proprietor of a shop, restaurant, hotel or guesthouse.

Excuse me, sir.	*o, dāi*	यो दाइ
Excuse me, madam.	*o, didi*	यो दिदि
Please come here.	*yahā̃ āunuhos*	यहाँ आउनुहोस्
proprietor	*sāhu-ji/sāhu-ni*	साहुजि (m)/ साहुनी (f)

Some Useful Phrases

Where are you going?
  tapāī̃ kahā̃ jānu huncha? तपाई कहाँ जानुहुन्छ ?
Where do you live/are you staying?
  tapāī̃ kahā̃ basnu huncha? तपाई कहाँ बस्नुहुन्छ ?
How are you (informal)?
  ke cha? के छ ?
Fine.
  thikcha ठीक छ
How are things?
  hāl khabar ke cha? हालखबर के छ ?
Okay, not bad.
  thikai cha ठीकै छ
Have you eaten?
  khānā khānu bhayo? खाना खानु भयो ?
I hope we meet again!
  pheri bhetaũlā! फेरी भेटौंला !

Note that when addressing someone by name, the Nepalis usually add the suffix *-ji* (or sometimes *-ju*) to the name as a sign of respect or affection.

Ram, where are you going?
rām-ji, tapāī kahā̃ jānu huncha? रामजी, तपाई कहाँ जानुहुन्छ ?

Body Language & Etiquette

Nepali social behaviour is different from that of most other cultures. Be sensitive to how people around you are acting, and you won't embarrass yourself too often! Nepalis will not usually be offended if a foreigner mistakenly behaves in a culturally inappropriate way.

Nepali people of all ethnic groups are very modest, and will feel uncomfortable around female or male tourists dressed revealingly. The Nepalis do not usually show their legs and men don't go without a shirt, even in hot weather. It is still much more acceptable for women to wear skirts than pants or shorts. Should you find it necessary to wash or bathe in public, be as discreet as possible, and keep at least some clothing on.

Touching someone with your feet or legs is insulting, and to apologise you should touch your hand to their arm or body and then touch your head. It is also considered bad manners to step over someone's outstretched legs, so withdraw your legs when someone is walking past. Open displays of affection between couples and even hand-holding are distasteful to the Nepalis. Don't be surprised, though, if you see men and boys walking with arms around each other's shoulders or even holding hands, and women walking arm-in-arm.

Tips & Gift-Giving

Small gifts for particular favours or tipping special service may be appropriate. If you want to give, try to assess real needs and give food, clothing or books, rather than money, sweets or cigarettes. It may be more appropriate to make a donation to a conservation or other project in the area, or to place money in a temple or monastery donation-box, so that informed local residents can decide where money is most needed.

Useful Tip

Consonants followed by an 'h' are aspirated. This means they are pronounced with an extra puff of air, like the 'th' in 'hothouse' or the 'ph' in 'haphazard'.

Common Expressions

No worries.	*bhaihālchani*	भईहाल्छनी
There's no point.	*matlab chaina*	मतलब छैन
Who cares?	*kolāi ke matlab?*	कोलाई के मतलब ?
Get lost!	*bhāg!*	भाग !

That's for sure.
  pakkā ho ho — पक्का हो हो

You're joking, aren't you?
  khyāl gareko holā, hoina? — ख्याल गरेको होला, होईन ?

Have a good rest.
  rāmro sanga basnuhos — राम्रो सँग बस्नुहोस

Have a good/safe trip home.
  rāmro sanga jānuhos — राम्रो सँग जानुहोस

What's to be done?
  ke garne? — के गर्ने ?

Small Talk

Top 10 Useful Phrases

Hello/Goodbye.	*namaste*	नमस्ते
Yes. (definition)	*ho*	हो
(location)	*cha*	छ
No. (definition)	*hoina*	होईन
(location)	*chaina*	छैन
Excuse me/Pardon?	*hajur?*	हजुर
I'm sorry/Excuse me.	*māph garnuhos*	माफ गर्नुहोस
How much is it?	*kati ho?*	कति हो ?
What is this/that?	*yo/tyo ke ho?*	यो / त्यो के हो ?

Where are you going?
    tapāī kahā̃ jāndai huncha?   तपाईं कहाँ जान्दै हुन्छ ?
Is this the way to ...?
    ... jāne bāto yehi ho?   ... जाने बाटो येहि हो ?
What's the matter?
    ke bhayo?   के भयो ?

Yes & No

There are several ways of answering 'Yes' or 'No' to questions. As in English, nodding means 'Yes' and a sideways shake of the head means 'No'. However, Nepalis slightly tilt the head and shrug the shoulders to indicate agreement, for instance, during bargaining. Don't mistake this for a 'No'. 'Yes/No' questions are also commonly answered by repeating the main verb in the affirmative or negative (see Grammar, page 23).

cha is used to confirm where something is, eg ' Is Gita there?', 'Yes *(cha)*, Gita is there.'

Yes. (agreement)	*hajur*	हजुर
(definition)	*ho*	हो
(location)	*cha*	छ
(permitted)	*huncha*	हुन्छ
No. (definition)	*hoina*	होइन
(location)	*chaina*	छैन
OK. (polite)	*huncha*	हुन्छ
(very polite)	*hās*	हास

..., isn't it/aren't they?
   ..., ho ki hoina?   हो कि होइन ?

Language Difficulties

Do you speak English?
   tapāī angreji bolna
   saknu huncha?   तपाई अंग्रेजि बोल्न सक्नुहुन्छ ?
I understand/I understood.
   ma bujhchu/maile bujhē   म बुझ्छु / मैले बुझें

SMALL TALK

I didn't understand.
maile bujhina
मैले बुझीन

Please say it again.
pheri bhannuhos
फेरी भन्नुहोस

Please speak more slowly.
bistārai bolnuhos
बिस्तारै बोल्नुहोस

Please write that down.
malāi tyo kurā lekh dinuhos
मलाई त्यो कुरा लेखदिनुहोस

I will look (for it) in this book.
ma yo kitābmā herchu
म यो किताबमा हेर्छु

Please wait a minute.
ekchin parkhanuhos
एकछिन पर्खनुहोस

How do you say ...?
... lāi ke bhancha?
... लाई के भन्छ ?

I know/don't know.
malāi thāhā cha/chaina
मलाई थाहा छ /छैन

I only speak a little Nepali.
ma ali ali nepāli bolchu
म अलि अलि नेपालि बोल्छु

Do you speak ...?
tapāī̃ ... ko bhāsā bolnu huncha?
तपाई ...को भाषा बोल्नुहुन्छ ?

I speak ...	*ma ... bhāsā bolchu*	म ... भाषा बोल्छु
English	*angreji (bhāsā)*	अंग्रेजि (भाषा)
French	*phrenc (bhāsā)*	फ्रेन्च (भाषा)
Hindi	*hindi*	हिन्दी
Bengali	*bangāli*	बंगालि
Tibetan	*tibetan*	तिबेतन

SMALL TALK

Indonesian	*indonesiyā*	ईण्डोनेसिया
Chinese	*cāiniz*	चाइनिज
Japanese	*jāpāniz*	जापानिज
German	*jarman*	जर्मन
Dutch	*dac*	डच

Meeting People

It is very easy to strike up a conversation with the Nepalis, and you'll be asked all sorts of questions about how you like Nepal, where you come from, your family, job and so on.

My name is ...
   mero nām ... ho   मेरो नाम ... हो
What is your name?
   tapāīko nām ke ho?   तपाईंको नाम के हो ?
Where do you come from?
   tapāīko ghar kahā̃ cha?   तपाईंको घर कहाँ छ ?

Where do you live/are you staying?
tapāī̃ kahā̃ basnu huncha? तपाईं कहाँ बस्नुहुन्छ ?

This is my friend.
yo mero sāthi ho यो मेरो साथि हो

His/Her name is ...
wahā̃ko nām ... ho वहाँको नाम ... हो

Please introduce yourself.
tapāī̃ko paricaya garnuhos तपाईंको परिचय गर्नुहोस

I'm here on holiday.
ma yahā̃ bidāmā ghumna āyako म यहाँ बिदामा घुम्न आयको

I'm here on business.
ma yahā̃ byāpār garna āyako म यहाँ ब्यापार गर्न आयको

Do you live here?
tapāī̃ yahā̃ basnu huncha? तपाईं यहाँ बस्नुहुन्छ ?

I like Nepal.
malāi nepāl man parcha मलाई नेपाल मनपर्छ

I like it here.

Nationalities

What country are you from?
tapāī̃ kun desh bāta āunu bhayako? तपाईं कुन देशबाट आउनु भयको ?

I'm from ...	*mero desh ... ho*	मेरो देश ... हो
Africa	*aphrikā*	अफ्रीका
Australia	*astreliyā*	अष्ट्रेलीया
Bangladesh	*banglādesh*	बँगलादेश

Belgium	*beljiyam*	बेल्जीयम
Britain	*belāyat*	बेलायट
Burma (Myanmar)	*barmā*	बर्मा
Canada	*kyānādā*	क्यानाडा
China	*cin*	चीन
Egypt	*misra*	मिस्र
France	*phrāns*	फ़्रान्स
Germany	*jarman*	जर्मन
Greece	*grunān*	ग्रूनान
Holland	*halāind*	हलाण्ड
India	*hindustān/bhārat*	हिन्दुस्तान / भारत
Indonesia	*indonesiyā*	इण्डोनेसीया
Iran	*irān*	ईरान
Ireland	*āyarlāind*	आयरलाईण्ड
Israel	*ijarāil*	ईजराईल
Italy	*itāli*	ईटाली
Japan	*jāpān*	जापान
Malaysia	*mālesiyā*	मालेशिया
Nepal	*nepāl*	नेपाल
New Zealand	*nyu jilāind*	न्यूजिलाईण्ड
Pakistan	*pākistān*	पाकिस्तान
Russia	*rus*	रूस
Spain	*ispen*	ईस्पेन
Sri Lanka	*sri lankā*	श्रीलंका
Taiwan	*cin janabādi ganatantra*	चीन जनबादि गनतन्त्र
Thailand	*thāilāind*	थाईलाईण्ड
Tibet	*tibet/bhot*	तिबेत / भोत

Turkey	*tarki*	टर्कि
the USA	*amerikā*	अमेरिका
Vietnam	*bhetnām*	भेटनाम

Age

How old are you?
  tapāī̃ kati barsa bhayo?   तपाईं कति बर्ष भयो ?
  tapāī̃ko umer kati bhayo?   तपाईंको उमेर कति भयो ?

I'm ... years old	*ma ... barsa bhayo*	म ... बर्ष भयो
18	*athāra*	अठार
35	*pentis*	पेंतीस

Occupations

What is your occupation?
  tapāī̃ko peshā ke ho?   तपाईंको पेशा के हो ?
Where do you work?
  tapāī̃ kahā̃ kām garnu   तपाईं कहाँ काम गर्नुहुन्छ ?
  huncha?
How do you enjoy your work?
  tapāī̃ko kām kasto lāgyo?   तपाईंको काम कस्तो लाग्यो ?
I (enjoy/don't enjoy) my work.
  mero kām (ramāilo cha/   मेरो काम (रमाईलो छ /
  rāmro chaina)   राम्रो छैन) ।

I'm a/an ...	*ma ... hū̃*	म ... हुँ
actor/artist	*kalākār*	कलाकार
architect	*vāstukār*	वास्तुकार
businessperson	*byāpāri*	ब्यापारी

clerk	*kārindā*	कारिन्दा
dancer	*nācne mānche*	नाच्ने मान्छे
doctor	*dāktar*	डाक्टर
engineer	*injiniyar*	इन्जिनियर
factory worker	*kārakhānāko majdur*	कारखानाको मजदुर
farmer	*kisān*	किसान
gardener	*māli*	माली
jeweller	*juhāri*	जुहारी
journalist	*patrakār*	पत्रकार
lawyer	*wakil*	वकील
musician	*sangitkār*	सँगीतकार
nurse	*dhāi*	धाई
office worker	*karmacāri*	कर्मचारी
painter	*citrakār*	चित्रकार
police officer	*prahari*	प्रहरी
priest	*pujāri*	पुजारी
scientist	*baigyānik*	बैज्ञानिक
secretary	*sacib*	सचिब
soldier	*sipāhi*	सिपाही
student	*bidyārthi*	बिद्यार्थी
tailor	*sujikār*	सुचिकार
teacher	*sichek*	शिक्षक
traveller	*yātri*	यात्री
unemployed	*kām nabhayako mānche*	काम नभयको मान्छे
waiter	*berā*	बेरा
writer	*lekhak*	लेखक

Religion

What is your religion?
tapāī kun dharma
mānnu huncha?

तपाईं कुन धर्म मान्नुहुन्छ ?

I am ...	*ma ... mānchu*	म ... मान्छु
Buddhist	*buddha dharma*	बुद्ध धर्म
Christian	*isāi dharma*	ईसाई धर्म
Hindu	*hindu dharma*	हिन्दु धर्म

I am Jewish.
ma yahudi hū̃

म यहुदि हुँ

I am a Muslim.
ma musalmān hū̃

म मुसलमान हुँ

I'm not religious.
ma kunai dharma māndina

म कुनै धर्म मान्दिन

Family

Forms of Address

The Nepali use kinship terms not only with their family but also with friends and even strangers, including foreigners. These terms are used far more commonly than names, so get used to calling people 'brother' and 'sister', and receiving the same in return. The term you use depends on whether the person is older or younger than you. Terms used for older people are generally more polite.

father	*buwā*	बुवा
mother	*āmā*	आमा
grandfather	*bāje*	बाजे
grandmother	*bajyai*	बजै
elder brother	*dāi*	दाइ
elder sister	*didi*	दिदी
younger brother	*bhāi*	भाइ
younger sister	*bahini*	बहिनी

Other Family Terms

brothers	*dājubhāi*	दाजुभाइ
children	*chorāchori*	छोराछोरी
daughter	*chori*	छोरी
family	*paribār*	परिबार
husband		
(own)	*logne*	लोग्ने
(someone else's)	*srimān*	श्रीमान
sisters	*didibahini*	दिदीबहिनी
son	*chorā*	छोरा
wife		
(own)	*swāsni*	स्वास्नी
(someone else's)	*srimati*	श्रीमति

Some Useful Phrases

Are you married?
  tapāīko bibāha bhayo?   तपाईंको बिबाह भयो ?
I am married/not married.
  mero bibāha bhayo/bhayo   मेरो बिबाह भयो / भयो छैन
  chaina

Is your husband/wife here?
*tapāīko srimān/srimati
yahā̃ hunu huncha?*

तपाईंको श्रीमान / श्रीमति
यहाँ हुनुहुन्छ ?

Do you have a boyfriend/
girlfriend.
tapāīko premi/premikā cha?

तपाईंको प्रेमि / प्रेमिका छ ?

Do you have any children?
tapāīko chorāchori chan?

तपाईंको छोराछोरी छन् ?

I don't have any children.
mero chorāchori chainan

मेरो छोराछोरी छैनन

How many children do you
have?
*tapāīko chorāchori kati
janā chan?*

तपाईंको छोराछोरी कति
जना छन् ?

I have two children.
  mero dui janā chorāchori chan
मेरो दुईजना छोराछोरी छन

I have a daughter/son.
  mero ek janā chori/chorā cha
मेरो एकजना छोरी / छोरा छ

How many in your family?
  tapāīko paribārmā kati janā chan?
तपाईंको परिबारमा कति जना छन ?

Are your parents alive?
  tapāīko āmā, buwā ahile samma jiundai hunu huncha?
तपाईंको आमा, बुवा अहिले सम्म जिउँदै हुनुहुन्छ ?

How many brothers do you have?
  tapāīko dājubhāi kati janā chan?
तपाईंको दाजुभाइ कति जना छन ?

How many sisters do you have?
  tapāīko didibahini kati janā chan?
तपाईंको दिदीबहिनी कति जना छन ?

Feelings

How do you feel?
  tapāīlāi kasto cha?
तपाईंलाई कस्तो छ ?

Are you happy/sad?
  tapāī khusi/dukhi hunu huncha?
तपाईं खुसी / दुखि हुनुहुन्छ ?

I feel/don't feel ...	*malāi ... lāgyo/ lāgena*	मलाई ... लाग्यो/ लागेन
angry	*ris*	रिस
annoyed	*dikka*	दि
cold	*jād̲o*	जाडो
drunk	*raksi*	रक्सी
happy	*khusi*	खुसी
hot	*garmi*	गर्मी
hungry	*bhok*	भोक
in a hurry	*hatār*	हतार
lost	*harāuna*	हराउन
right	*thik*	ठीक
sad/sorry	*dukhi*	दुखी
scared	*d̲ar*	डर
sick	*birāmi*	बिरामि
sleepy	*nindrā*	निन्द्रा
thirsty	*tirkhā*	तिर्खा
tired	*thakāi*	थकाइ
windblown	*hāwā*	हावा
worried	*pir*	पिर
wrong	*bethik*	बेठिक

USEFUL TIP

Say it through the nose!

Nasal sounds are indicated by a tilde (~) over the vowel or by an 'n' or 'm' following it.

Opinions

I agree/disagree.
ma sahamat chu/chaina म सहमत छु/छैन
Do you agree?
tapāī sahamat hunu huncha? तपाई सहमत हुनुहुन्छ ?
What do you think?
tapāīko bicār ke cha? तपाईको बिचार के छ ?
I think that ...
mero bicārmā ... मेरो बचारमा ...
That's my opinion.
tehi mero bicār ho तेहि मेरो बिचार हो
Do you like it?
tapāīlāī yo man parcha? तपाईलाई यो मनपर्छ ?
I like/don't like it.
malāi yo man parcha/ मलाई यो मनपर्छ/मनपर्दैन
man pardaina
It's important/not important.
mahatwa purna cha/chaina महत्वपुर्ण छ/छैन
That's true/not true.
tyo sānco ho/hoina त्यो साँचो हो/होईन
This is good/bad.
yo rāmro cha/kharāb cha यो राम्रो छ/खराब छ

Making Conversation

How do you like Nepal?
tapāīlāī nepāl kasto तपाईलाई नेपाल कस्तो लाग्यो ?
lāgyo?
I like Nepal a lot.
malāi nepāl ekdam rāmro मलाई नेपाल एकदम राम्रो
lāgyo लाग्यो

We're just friends.
hāmi sāthi mātrai hau̐ हामि साथि मात्रै हौं

We're relatives.
hāmi nātedār hau̐ हामि नातेदार हौं

What nice weather (isn't it)?
kasto rāmro mausam, hoina ra? कस्तो राम्रो मौसम, होइन र ?

What a cute baby!
kasto rāmro baccā! कस्तो राम्रो बच्चा !

You're lucky.
tapāī bhāgyamāni तपाई भाग्यमानि

What is your caste/ethnic group?
tapāīko jāt ke ho? तपाईको जात के हो ?

Interests

Do you like ...?
tapāīlāī ... man parcha? तपाईलाई ... मनपर्छ ?

I like/don't like ...	*malāi ... man parcha/pardaina*	मलाई ... मनपर्छ / मनपर्दैन
dancing	*nācna*	नाच्न
seeing films	*calacitra herna*	चलचित्र हेर्न
shopping	*kinmel garna*	किनमेल गर्न
music	*sangit sunna*	संगीत सुन्न
playing games	*khel garna*	खेल गर्न
playing/watching sport	*khelkud khelna/ herna*	खेलकुद खेल्न / हेर्न

SMALL TALK

reading	*padhna*	पढ्न
travelling	*yātrā garna*	यात्रा गर्न
watching TV	*telibhijan herna*	टेलिभिजन हेर्न
playing cards	*tās khelna*	तास खेल्न

It's fun (to do ...).

| *(... garna) majjā lāgcha* | (...गर्न) मज्जा लाग्छ |

Special Occasions

Best wishes!	*subha kāmanā!*	शुभकामना !
Happy birthday!	*janma dinko subha kāmanā!*	जन्म दिनको शुभकामना !
Congratulations!	*badhāi cha!*	बधाई छ !
Good luck!	*saphalhos!*	सफलहोस !
(a blessing)	*bhāgyamāni!* (literally 'lucky')	भाग्यमानि !

USEFUL TIP

Give it a kick!

When you see a double consonant, it needs an extra kick, so pronounce it forcefully.

Interjections

English	Romanization	Devanagari
Hey you!	*e dāi!*	ए दाइ !
Damn!	*het terikā!*	हेट्रीका !
How surprising!	*kasto gajjab!*	कस्तो गज्जब !
Bravo/Well done!	*shyābās!*	श्याबास !
O God!	*hāre!*	हारे !
	he bhagwān!	हे भगवान !
No.	*ahã*	अहँ !
Shut up/Be quiet!	*cup!*	चुप !
Ow/Ouch!	*aiyyā!*	अँय्या !
Tut tut!		
(disapproval)	*chi chi!*	छि छि !
(wonder, pleasure)	*ahā!*	अहा !

Some Useful Phrases

Just wait a moment.
ekchin parkhanuhos एकछिन पर्खनुहोस

What are you doing?
tapāī ke gardaihunu huncha? तपाईं के गर्दैहुनुहुन्छ ?

It's nothing/It doesn't matter.
kehi chaina केहि छैन

You're right.
  *tapāīle **t**hik bhannu bhayo*   तपाईंले ठीक भन्नु भयो
Really?
  sāncai?   साँचै ?
It's enough.
  pugcha   पुग्छ

Getting Around

Finding Your Way

The Nepalis are helpful in giving directions, and may even offer to escort you to your destination. It isn't difficult to get lost as you walk along winding alleys and trails, but it's the best way to see interesting local scenes.

How do I get to ...?
   ... kasari jāne?   ... कसरी जाने ?
Could you tell me where ... is?
   ... kahā̃ cha?   ... कहाँ छ ?
Is this the way to ...?
   yo bāto ... jāne bāto ho?   यो बाटो ... जाने बाटो हो ?
Is there another way to get there?
   arko kasari jāne?   अर्को कसरी जाने ?
Is it far from here?
   yahā̃ bāta tāḍhā cha?   यहाँबाट टाढा छ ?
Can I walk there?
   hī̃dera jāna sakinchu?   हिंडेर जान सकिन्छु ?

Is it difficult to get there?
   jāna gāhro cha?   जान गाहो छ ?

What ... is this?	*yo kun ... ho?*	यो कुन ... हो ?
road	*bāto*	बाटो
place	*thāū̃*	ठाउँ

Directions

across	*pāri*	पारी
along	*hundai*	हुन्दै
back/behind	*pachādi*	पछाडि
beside	*cheumā*	छेउमा
down/below	*tala*	तल
in front of	*agādi*	अगाडि
inside/into	*bhitra*	भित्र
left	*bāyā̃*	बायाँ
middle/centre	*bic*	बिच
on	*mā*	मा
out/outside	*bāhira*	बाहिर
over/above	*māthi*	माथि
over there	*u tyahā̃*	उ त्यहाँ
right	*dāyā̃*	दायाँ
side	*cheu*	छेउ
towards	*tira*	तिर
up there	*u māthi*	उ माथि

Transport

There are no trains in Nepal, and much of the country can only be reached by walking or flying. In towns, rickshaws, autorickshaws and taxis are commonly available and inexpensive. Apart from buses, you should bargain over the cost for a particular journey, especially with taxi drivers, who may refuse to use their meters. Drivers are also notorious for being unable to change large bills and not carrying any small change, so try to keep some with you.

Town buses are very cheap but always extremely crowded and slow. Country buses, especially tourist ones, aren't so bad. Taxis and chauffeur-driven cars are readily available for longer trips, but are expensive, as are motorbikes for hire. Bicycles are the cheapest form of urban transport and often the most convenient, as taxis after dark are difficult to find and charge twice, or even more, the meter fare.

Is a/an ... available? *yahā̃ ... pāincha?* यहाँ ... पाइन्छ ?

autorickshaw	*tyāmpu*	त्याम्पु
bicycle	*sāikal*	साइकल
bus	*bas*	बस
motor car	*motar*	मोटर
motorcycle	*motar sāikal*	मोटर साइकल
rickshaw	*rikshā*	रिक्सा
taxi	*tyāksi*	त्याक्सी
vehicle	*gādi*	गाडि

Buying Tickets

Where do they sell (bus) tickets?
   (basko) tikat kahā̃ beccha? (बसको) टिकट कहाँ बेच्छ ?
Where can I buy a (plane) ticket?
   (plenko) tikat kahā̃ kinne? (प्लेनको) टिकट कहाँ किन्ने ?
I want to go to ...
   ma ... jānchu म ... जान्छु
How much is it to go to ...?
   ... ko lāgi kati paisā lāgcha? ... को लागि कति पैसा लाग्छ ?
Is there a flight to ...?
   ... mā plen jāncha? ... मा प्लेन जान्छ ?
I want a one-way/return
ticket.
   jāne/jāne-āune tikat जाने/जाने-आउने टिकट
   dinuhos दिनुहोस
How long does the trip take?
   pugnalāi kati samay lāgcha? पुग्नलाई कति समय लाग्छ ?

What time does it ...?	*kati baje ...?*	कति बजे ...?
arrive	*pugne*	पुग्ने
leave	*jāne*	जाने
return	*pharkane*	फर्कने

Bicycle Hire

How much is a bicycle per (hour/day)?
    sāikal (ghanṭāko/dinko) kati ho?
साईकल (घण्टाको / दिनको) कति हो ?

I'd like to hire a bicycle for ...	*malāi ... kolāgi euṭā sāikal bhāndāmā cāhiyo*	मलाई ... कोलागि एउटा साईकल भौंडामा चाहियो
one day	*ek din*	एक दिन
two days	*dui din*	दुई दिन
one week	*ek haptā*	एक हप्ता

Bus

Does this bus go to ...?
    yo ... jāne bas ho?
यो ... जाने बस हो ?
Where does this bus go?
    yo bas kahā̃ jāne?
यो बस कहाँ जाने ?
Is the bus completely full?
    bas bharyo?
बस भर्यो ?

Are there any stops?
katai rokcha?
कतै रोक्छ ?

Will it be on time?
samaymā pugcha?
समयमा पुग्छ ?

Is that seat taken?
yahā̃ kohi mānche cha?
यहाँ कोहि मान्छे छ ?

Please stop (the bus) when
we get to ...
... *āye pachi (bas) roki dinuhos*
... आये पछि (बस) रोकिदिनुहोस

I want to get off here.
ma yahā̃ orlinchu
म यहाँ ओर्लिन्छु

When is the ... trip? ... *yātrā kahile jāne?*... यात्रा कहिले जाने ?

next	*arko*	अर्को
first	*pahilā*	पहिला
last	*antim*	अन्तिम

Taxi & Rickshaw

Can you take me to ...?
... *mā lānu huncha?*
... मा लानुहुन्छ ?

For two people?
dui janāko lāgi?
दुईजनाको लागि ?

Does that include the
luggage?
sāmān samet garera?
सामान समेत गरेर ?

How much do I owe you?
  kati paisā dinu parcha?   कति पैसा दिनुपर्छ ?
Is it far from here?
  yahā̃bāta ke tāḍhā cha?   यहाँबाट के टाढा छ ?
It is near here.
  najik cha   नजिक छ

Instructions

Go straight ahead.	*sidhā jānuhos*	सिधा जानुहोस
Turn left/right.	*bāyā̃/dāyā̃ modnuhos*	बायाँ / दायाँ मोइनुहोस
Drive slowly.	*bistārai hānknuhos*	बिस्तारै हाँ
Please hurry.	*chito garnuhos*	छिटो गर्नुहोस
Be careful!	*hos garnuhos!*	होस गर्नुहोस !
Stop!	*roknuhos!*	रो !
Keep going.	*jāndai garnuhos*	जान्दै गर्नुहोस

USEFUL TIP

Stretch it out!

A line (called a macron) over a vowel indicates
that it is a long vowel sound. Imagine the line is
stretching the sound out.

GETTING AROUND

Some Useful Words

address	*thegānā*	ठेगाना
arrival	*āgaman*	आगमण
boat	*dungā*	डुंगा
(to) cancel	*radda garnu*	रद्द गर्नु
(to) confirm	*pakkā garnu*	पक्का गर्नु
corner	*kunā*	कुना
customs	*bhansār*	भन्सार
departure	*prasthān*	प्रस्थान
early	*saberai*	सबेरै
fast	*chito*	छिटो
late	*dhilo*	ढिलो
map	*naksā*	नक्सा
reservation	*sancaya*	सँञ्चय
seat	*basne thāū*	बसने ठाउँ
ticket	*tikat*	टिकट
timetable	*samaya tālikā*	समय तालिका
tourist	*paryatak*	पर्यटक

Accommodation

In Kathmandu all types of accommodation are available, ranging from five-star hotels to small guesthouses with picturesque roof gardens, and tiny lodges with very basic facilities and rock-bottom prices.

Outside Kathmandu accommodation varies considerably. In towns and tourist centres, the range and prices are similar to those in the capital. In the countryside most hotels and lodges are modestly priced, but standards differ.

Accommodation on trekking routes can be particularly primitive, especially in remote areas. More popular trekking routes are nowadays lined with lodges offering (but not necessarily able to provide) all kinds of facilities, from hot water to Western-style food.

If you arrange for an evening meal on less popular trekking routes, the price quoted to you traditionally includes accommodation for the night, but do ask. If you are staying in one area for some time, most guesthouses don't mind if there's some food preparation in your room. Try to get a place near a local market, as fridges are a luxury item in Nepal and are rarely provided, even in expensive accommodation.

Finding Accommodation

Where is a ...?	... *kahã cha?*	... कहाँ छ ?
campsite	*shivir*	शिविर
guesthouse	*pāhunā ghar*	पाहुना घर
hotel	*hotel*	होटेल
lodge	*laj*	लज

What is the address?
thegānā ke ho?   ठेगाना के हो ?
Please write down the
address.
thegānā lekhnuhos   ठेगाना लेख्नुहोस

I'm looking for a ...	*ma ... khojeko*	म ... खोजेको
cheap lodge	*sasto laj*	सस्तो लज
good hotel	*rāmro hotel*	राम्रो होटेल
nearby hotel	*najik hotel*	नजिक होटेल
clean hotel	*saphā hotel*	सफा होटेल

At the Hotel
Checking In
Do you have any rooms?
kothā pāincha?   कोठा पाइन्छ ?
I have a reservation.
mero sancaya rākheko   मेरो सँञ्चय राखेको

I would like a ...	*ma ... cāhiyo*	म ... चाहियो
single room	*ek janāko lāgi*	एकजनाको लागि
double room	*dui janāko lāgi*	दुईजनाको लागि
	kothā	कोठा

I want a room	*malāi ... bhayako*	मलाई ... भयको
with ...	*kothā cāhiyo*	कोठा चाहियो
hot water	*tāto pāni*	तातो पानी
a window	*jhyāl*	झयाल

ACCOMMODATION

How much is it per night?
ek rātko, kati paisā ho?
एकरातको, कति पैसा हो ?

Does it include breakfast?
bihānako khānā samet ho?
बिहानको खाना समेत हो ?

Can I see the room?
kothā herna sakincha?
कोठा हेर्न सकिन्छ ?

Are there any others?
arko kothā pāincha?
अर्को कोठा पाईन्छ ?

Are there any cheaper rooms?
arko kunai sasto kothā cha?
अर्को कुनै सस्तो कोठा छ ?

Do you allow children?
baccā pani basnu huncha?
बच्चा पनि बस्नुहुन्छ ?

Is there a discount for children?
ke baccāko lāgi kam huncha?
के बच्चाको लागि कम हुन्छ ?

Does the hotel have a restaurant?
hotelmā bhojanālaya cha?
होटेलमा भोजनालय छ ?

Laundry

Is there somewhere to wash
clothes?
   lugā dhune thāū pāincha?   लुगाधुने ठाउँ पाईन्छ ?
Is there a laundry nearby?
   ke etā lugā dhune thāū   के एता लुगाधुने ठाउँ
   najik cha?   नजिक छ ?

Can I have this ...?   *yo lugā ...?*   यो लुगा ...?
   washed   *dhui dinuhos*   धुई दिनुहोस
   ironed   *istri lagāunuhos*   ईस्ट्री लगाउनुहोस

I need this clothing today/
tomorrow
   mero lugā āja/bholi   मेरो लुगा आज/भोलि
   cāhincha   चाहिन्छ
Is my laundry ready?
   mero lugā tayār bhayo?   मेरो लुगा तयार भयो ?

Requests

I have a request.
   eutā anurodh cha   एउटा अनुरोध छ

Please give me ...   *malāi ... dinuhos*   मलाई ... दिनुहोस
   bedding   *bichayaunā*   बिछयौना
   breakfast   *bihānako khānā*   बिहानको खाना
   a candle   *mainbatti*   मैनबत्ती
   a chair   *mec*   मेच
   a curtain   *pardā*   पर्दा
   a fan   *pankhā*   पंखा

Do you have a safe?
  tapāĩkahā̃ surachit
  thāũ cha?

तपाईंकहाँ सुरक्षित ठाउँ छ ?

Could I leave this to be
stored?
  yo chodna sakincha?

यो छोड्न सकिन्छ ?

Could I use the phone?
  ma phon garna sakchu?

म फोन गर्न स ?

Could someone look after
my child?
  mero baccālāi herna
  sakincha?

मेरो बच्चालाई हेर्न सकिन्छ ?

Please wake me up at ...
o'clock tomorrow morning.
   malāi bholi bihāna ... baje
   uthāunuhos

मलाई भोलि बिहान ... बजे उठाउनुहोस

Please clean the room.
   kothā saphā garnuhos

कोठा सफा गर्नुहोस

Please change the sheets.
   tannā phernuhos

तन्ना फेर्नुहोस

Do I leave my key at reception?
   sānco risepsanmā chodne?

साँचो रीसेप्सनमा छोड्ने ?

Complaints

Excuse me, there's a problem
with my room.
   o sāhuji, mero kothāmā
   samasyā bhayo

ओ साहुजि, मेरो कोठामा समस्या भयो

The window doesn't open/
close.
   jhyāl kholna/lāuna sakena

झ्याल खोल्न/लाउन सकेन

I've locked the key in my
room.
   sānco kothāmā paryo

सांचो कोठामा पर्यो

The toilet won't flush.
   shaucālaya kām gardaina

शौचालय काम गर्दैन

There's no (hot) water.
   (tāto) pāni chaina

(तातो) पानी छैन

The ... doesn't work.
   ... kām gardaina

... काम गर्दैन

Can you get this fixed?
   yo banāuna sakcha?

यो बनाउन सक्छ ?

I don't like this room.
malāi yo kothā man मलाई यो कोठा मनपर्दैन
pardaina

It's too ...	*dherai ... cha*	धेरै ... छ
small	*sāno*	सानो
cold/hot	*ciso/tāto*	चिसो / तातो
dark	*andhyāro*	अँध्यारो
noisy	*hallā*	हल्ला
expensive	*mahango*	महंगो

This room smells.
yo kothā ganāuncha यो कोठा गनाउन्छ

ACCOMMODATION

Checking Out

I would like to	*ma ... jānchu*	म ... जान्छु
check out ...		
now	*ahile*	अहिले
at noon	*bārha baje*	बाह्र बजे
tomorrow	*bholi*	भोलि

USEFUL TIP

Remember:
The Nepali 'c' is pronounced as the 'ch' in 'church', but a little less breathy.

Can I leave my bags here?
ke ma yahã̃ jholā chodna   के म यहाँ झोला छोड्न
sakincha?   सकिन्छ ?
I'd like to pay now.
ma ahile paisā tirchu   म अहिले पैसा तिर्छु

I'm coming back ...   *ma ... pharkinchu*   म ... फर्किन्छु
   in a few days   *kehi din pachi*   केहि दिन पछि
   in two weeks   *dui haptā pachi*   दुई हप्ता पछि

Some Useful Phrases

Is ... available?   *... pāincha?*   ... पाईन्छ ?
   a garden   *bagaincā*   बगैंचा
   food   *khānā*   खाना
   tea/coffee   *ciyā, kaphi*   चिया, कफी
   boiled water   *umāleko pāni*   उमालेको पानी

I'm staying for ...   *ma ... baschu*   म ... बस्छु
   three nights   *tin rāt*   तीन रात
   a week   *ek haptā*   एक हप्ता

I'm not sure how long I'll stay.
kati basne malāi thāhā chaina   कति बस्ने मलाई थाहा छैन
Where is the toilet?
shaucālaya kahã̃ cha?   शौचालय कहाँ छ ?
Is there hot water all day?
din bhari tāto pāni āuncha?   दिन भरी तातो पानी आउन्छ ?

Some Useful Words

address	*thegānā*	ठेगाना
apartment	*derā*	डेरा
babysitter	*baccā herne mānche*	बच्चा हेर्ने मान्छे
balcony	*bārdali*	बार्दली
basin/sink	*besan*	बेसन
(to) bathe/shower	*nuhāunu*	नुहाउनु
bathroom	*snān kaksha*	स्नान कक्ष
bed	*khāt*	खाट
blanket	*kambal*	कम्बल
candle	*mainbatti*	मैनबत्ती
chair	*mec*	मेच
cheap	*sasto*	सस्तो
(to) clean	*saphā (garnu)*	सफा (गर्नु)
cot	*khātiyā*	खाटिया
dark	*andhyāro*	अँध्यारो
dirty	*phohor*	फोहोर
electricity	*bijuli*	बिजुली
excluded	*bāhek*	बाहेक
expensive	*mahango*	महंगो
fan	*pankhā*	पंखा
fireplace	*agenu*	अगेनु
first name	*subha nām*	शुभनाम
heater	*hitar*	हिटर
hut	*jhupro*	झुप्रो
including	*samet*	समेत
key	*sānco*	साँचो

ACCOMMODATION

lightbulb	*cim*	चीम
lock	*cukul*	चुकुल
mattress	*dasanā*	डसना
mirror	*ainā*	ऐना
pillow	*sirāni*	सिरानी
plug (v)	*bujo lāunu*	बुजो लाउनु
quiet	*shānta*	शान्त
quilt	*sirak*	सिरक
room	*kothā*	कोठा
room number	*kothāko nambar*	कोठाको नम्बर
sheet	*tannā*	तन्ना
shower (n)	*snān*	स्नान
soap	*sābun*	साबुन
surname	*thar*	थर
tap/faucet	*dhārā*	धारा
toilet (flushing)	*bāthrum*	बाथरुम
(pit)	*carpi*	चर्पि
(public)	*shaucālaya*	शैचालय
toilet paper	*twāilet pepar*	टवाईलेट पेपर
towel/napkin/ handkerchief	*rumāl*	रुमाल
water	*pāni*	पानी
window	*jhyāl*	झ्याल

Around Town

I'm looking for ...   *ma ... khoji rahako*   म ... खोजी रहको
  a bank   *baink*   बैंङ्क
  the ... embassy   *... rājdutāvās*   ... राजदूतावास
  my hotel   *mero hotel*   मेरो होटेल
  the museum   *samgrahālaya*   संग्राहालय
  the police   *prahari*   प्रहरी
  the post office   *hulāk addā*   हुलाक अड्डा
  the tourism office   *paryatan kāryālaya*   पर्यटन कार्यालय

What time does it open/close?
  kati baje kholcha/banda   कति बजे खोल्छ/बन्द गर्छ ?
  garcha?

At the Embassy

Where can I extend my visa?
  bhisā kahā̃ thapnu?   भिसा कहाँ थप्नु ?
Please extend my visa for ...
days.
  malāi ... dinko lāgi arko   मलाई ... दिनको लागि अर्को
  bhisā dinuhos   भिसा दिनुहोस

79

When can I collect my
passport?

*mero rāhadāni kahile lina
āune?*

मेरो राहदानी कहिले लिन
आउने ?

At the Post Office

Nepal's postal service is not bad but posting anything in
letterboxes and even giving letters to your hotel can be risky.
Make sure you see the postal clerk cancel the stamps on your
mail. There aren't many post offices in Nepal and their hours are
short, so there are usually queues.

I want to send ...	... *pathāunu paryo*	... पठाउनु पर्यो
an aerogram	*hawāi patra*	हवाईपत्र
a letter	*citthi*	चिट्ठी
a parcel	*pulindā*	पूर्लिंदा
a telegram	*teligrām/tār*	टेलिग्राम / तार

Please give me some stamps.

malāi tikat dinuhos

मलाई टिकट दिनुहोस

How much is it to send
this to ...?

... mā kati lāgcha?

... मा कति लाग्छ ?

How much is it to send this by ...?	*yo ... kati paisā lāgcha?*	यो ... कति पैसा लाग्छ ?
airmail	*hawāi dāk garna*	हवाईडाक गर्न
ship	*jahāj bāta pathāuna*	जहाजबाट पठाउन

Telephone

In Nepali towns there are many small communications offices where you can make and receive phone calls, and send and receive faxes.

I want to call ...
  malāi ... phon garnu paryo   मलाई ... फोन गर्नुपर्‍यो

I want to make a reverse-
charge (collect) call to ...
  malāi yahā̃ bāta ... mā phon   मलाई यहाँबाट ...मा फोन
  garnu paryo, paisā tyahā̃   गर्नुपर्‍यो, पैसा त्यहाँबाट तिर्छ
  bāta tircha

The number is ...
  nambar ... ho   नम्बर ... हो

I want to speak for three
minutes.
  tin minet phon garchu   तीन मिनेट फोन गर्छु

How much is it per minute?
  minetko kati ho?   मिनेटको कति हो ?

Hello, do you speak English?
  namaste, angreji bolnu   नमस्ते, अँग्रेजी बोल्नुहुन्छ ?
  huncha?

Is ... there?
  ... cha?   ... छ ?

Yes (he/she is here).
  cha   छ

One moment.
  ek chin   एकछिन

We were cut off.
  lāin kātyo   लाईन काट्यो

I want to send a fax to ...
malāi phāks ... mā pathāunu
paryo

मलाई फ्याक्स ...मा पठाउनु
पर्‍यो

At the Bank

Exchange counters in Nepal, unlike many
other countries, don't normally charge more
than the bank rate, except for some expensive hotels. Be sure to keep all your exchange
receipts if you want to extend your visa or
re-exchange rupees at the airport when you
leave.

I want to change some money.
paisā alikati sāṭnu paryo

पैसा अलिकति साट्नुपर्‍यो

I'd like to change this into
Nepali rupees.
yo nepāli rupaiyẫmā sāti
dinuhos

यो नेपाली रुपैर्‍यामा साटी
दिनुहोस

What is the exchange rate
today?
āja sāṭne reṭ kati cha?

आज साट्ने रेट कति छ ?

How many rupees per dollar?
ek dalarko kati ho?

एक डलरको कति हो ?

Can I have money sent here
from my bank?
mero baink bāṭa paisā
yahẫ āuncha?

मेरो बैङ्कबाट पैसा
यहाँ आउन्छ ?

How long will it take?
pugna kati samay lāgcha?

पुग्न कति समय लाग्छ ?

I'm expecting some money from ...

... bāta paisā apechā garchu ...बाट पैसा अपेक्षा गर्छु

Has my money arrived (yet)?

mero paisā āyo? मेरो पैसा आयो ?

Please give me smaller change for this note.

yallāi khudra paisā dinuhos यलाई खुद्र पैसा दिनुहोस

Sightseeing

Nepal is full of fascinating historical and religious sights, and in many places people will be happy to show you around and give background information. Most Nepalis don't mind being photographed, but be sensitive and always ask first, especially during religious ceremonies or bathing. There isn't much nightlife in Kathmandu but the casinos stay open late. People tend to stay home after dark, but the streets are generally quite safe at night.

When visiting temples, dress modestly and remove your shoes. Signs at Hindu temples will also ask you to remove any leather objects, such as belts, before entering the compound. Photography may be permitted, but look for signs and ask if unsure.

Where is the tourism office?

paryatan kāryālaya kahā̃ cha? पर्यटन कार्यालय कहाँ छ ?

Where can I hire a guide?

malāi ghumāune mānche kahā̃ pāincha? मलाई घुमाउने मान्छे कहाँ पाइन्छ ?

How much is the entry fee?

prabesh shulka kati ho? प्रबेश शुल्क कति हो ?

How much is it to go inside?
  bhitra jānalāi kati paisā
  lāgcha?

भित्र जानलाई कति पैसा
लाग्छ ?

What's that ...?	*tyo ... ke ho?*	त्यो ... के हो ?
building	*bhawan*	भवन
monument	*smārak*	स्मारक
temple		
(Hindu)	*mandir*	मन्दिर
(Buddhist)	*stupā*	ईस्तुपा

How old is it?
  kati purāno bhayo?

कति पुरानो भयो ?

Who built it?
kasle banāyeko?   कसले बनायेको ?

Is it OK to take photos?
tasbir khicnu huncha?   तस्बीर खिच्नुहुन्छ ?

May I take your photo?
tapāīko tasbir khicnu huncha?   तपाईंको तस्बीर खिच्नुहुन्छ ?

I will send you the photo.
tasbir tapāīlāi pathāunchu   तस्बीर तपाईंलाई पठाउन्छु

I will send you a letter.
tapāīlāi citthi pathāunchu   तपाईंलाई चिठ्ठी पठाउन्छु

Please write down your name
and address.
*tapāīko nām ra thegānā
lekhnuhos*   तपाईंको नाम र ठेगाना
लेख्नुहोस

Please take my photo.
mero tasbir khicnuhos   मेरो तस्बीर खिच्नुहोस

Some Useful Words

ancient	*prācin*	प्राचिन
cremation	*dāhasanskār*	दाहसंस्कार
cremation ghat (platform)	*ghāt*	घाट
cultural show	*sānskritik pradarshan*	सांस्कृीतिक प्रदर्शन
factory	*kārakhānā*	कारखाना
gardens	*bagaincā*	बगैंचा
god/goddess	*deutā*	देवटा
library	*pustakālaya*	पुस्तकालय
market	*bajār*	बजार

monastery	*gumbā*	गुम्बा
monument	*smārak*	स्मारक
mosque	*masjid*	मस्जिद
old city	*purāno shahar*	पुरानो शहर
pagoda	*gajur*	गजुर
palace	*darbār*	दरबार
religion/philosophy	*dharma*	धर्म
restaurant	*bhojanālaya*	भोजनालय
statue/idol	*murti*	मर्ति
university	*bishwa bidyālaya*	बिश्वबिद्यालय
zoo	*cidiyā khānā*	चिडियाखाना

Trekking

Eight of the world's 14 highest mountains are found in Nepal, and its northern frontier is bordered by the mighty Himalaya (pronounced with the stress on the second, not third, syllable). So Nepal is well known for having some of the best trekking in the world.

Most trekking areas are remote, and the Nepalis who live in the mountains and high valleys are more traditional than those in towns. They are devout and more observant of local customs, which are deeply rooted in their religion, a harmonious mixture of Hinduism, Buddhism and ancient Tantrism. As you walk along you will come across holy buildings, stupas (white domes with prayer flags) and walls of prayer stones. Always keep these on your right as you pass.

Along the trails, and in villages, you will come across a kind of community resting place or meeting place, made by building rocks and stones into a comfortable seating area at the base of a shady tree – often a very large tree. This is called a *cautārā* and the locals will be more than happy for you to join them there. *Cautārās* are easy to recognise and are commonly referred to when giving directions.

Nepali is not usually the main language spoken by the people you meet while trekking, but most will know it. It is well worth the small expense of hiring a guide or porter *(bhariyā)*, as you will learn much more about the area, and will probably be invited into their home.

Even if you choose relatively remote and less populous trekking routes, you'll have few difficulties with language, porters, equipment or accommodation. However, foodstuffs can be scarce so be prepared to take along whatever you need. Villagers will often offer to let you share their meal and home, but never enter a house uninvited. And remember that the fireplace is sacred, so don't throw rubbish into it.

All villages have a communal pit toilet *(carpi)* which trekkers are welcome to use. The Nepalis don't use toilet paper (they don't have any) and think it's pretty strange. They use a waterjug *(lotā)* and their left hand, which is naturally not used for anything else such as giving or receiving, or shaking hands!

Hiring Porters

Excuse me, will you go with me to ...?

    e, tapāī masanga ... samma jāne?   ए, तपाई मसंग ... सम्म जाने ?

How many days will it take,
there and back?
    jāna, āuna, kati din lāgcha?   जान, आउन, कति दिन लाग्छ ?
How much are you asking?
    tapāī kati bhannu huncha?   तपाई कति भन्नुहुन्छ ?
With/without food?
    khānā khāyara/nakhāyara?   खाना खायर / नखायर ?
With/without a load?
    bhāri cha/chaina?   भारी छ / छैन ?
I'll give you ... rupees per
day.
    ma tapāīlāi dinko ...   म तपाईलाई दिनको ...
    rupaiyā̃ dinchu   रुपैयाँ दिन्छु
We'll leave at ...
    hāmi ... jānchaũ   हामि ... जान्छैं
We'll meet at (place).
    ... mā bhetne   ... मा भेट्ने

Asking Directions

When asking how long it takes to reach a destination, remember
that locals travel faster than you! Distance is often measured in
kos: one *kos* is about three kilometres. *Dui kos* (literally 'two
kos') is an expression meaning 'not too far'.

Which is the way to Lukla?
    luklā jāne bāto kun ho?   लुक्ला जाने बाटो कुन हो ?

TREKKING

What is the next village?
āune gāūko nām ke ho?
आउने गाउंको नाम के हो ?

Is this the way to ...?
... jāne bāto yehi ho?
... जाने बाटो येहि हो ?

How far is it to ...?
... mā kati tāḍhā parcha?
...मा कति टाढा पर्छ ?

How many hours/days?
kati ghaṇtā/din?
कति घण्टा/दिन ?

Which direction?
kun dishā?
कुन दिशा ?

Where have you come from?
kahā̃bāta āunu bhayeko?
कहाँबाट आउनु भयेको ?

From Pokhara.
pokharā bāta
पोखराबाट

It takes us three hours.
hāmilāi tin ghaṇtā lāgcha
हामिलाई तीन घण्टा लाग्छ

For you it will take four to
five hours.
*tapāīlāi cār-pānc ghaṇtā
lāgcha*
तपाईंलाई चार-पाँच घण्टा
लाग्छ

north
uttar
उत्तर

east
purba
पूर्व

west
pascim
पश्चिम

south
dachin
दक्षिण

left	*bayã*	बायाँ
right	*dayã*	दायाँ
this side	*wāri*	वारी
that side	*pāri*	पारी
level	*samma*	सम्म
upward	*māstira*	मास्तिर
uphill	*ukālo*	उकालो
steep uphill	*thādo*	ठाडो
downward	*talatira*	तलतिर
downhill	*orālo*	ओरालो
steep downhill	*bhirālo*	भिरालो
straight ahead	*sidhā*	सिधा
a little	*ali ali*	अलि अलि

Along the Way

Where can I spend the night?
  bās basna kahā̃ pāincha?   बास बस्न कहाँ पाईन्छ ?
There are three of us.
  hāmi tin janā chaũ   हामि तीन जना छौं
Do you provide meals?
  khānā pāincha ki?   खाना पाईन्छ की ?
What kind of food?
  ke khānā pāincha?   के खाना पाईन्छ ?

Please ask about ...	... *bāre sodhnuhos*	... बारे सोध्नुहोस
boiled water	*umāleko pāni*	उमालेको पानी
bread	*roti*	रोटी
food	*khānā*	खाना
tea	*ciyā*	चिया

TREKKING

Please give me ...	*malāi ... dinuhos*	मलाई ... दिनुहोस
rice beer	*cyāng*	च्याङ
cooked rice	*bhāt*	भात
lentils	*dāl*	दाल
shelter	*bās*	बास
tobacco	*surti*	सुर्ति
vegetables	*tarakāri*	तरकारी
rakshi (local spirit)	*rakshi*	रक्सी

Where is the ...?	*... kahā̃ cha?*	... कहाँ छ ?
bridge	*pul*	पुल
inn	*bhatti*	भट्टी
cautārā (resting place)	*cautārā*	चौतारा
statue	*murti*	मूर्ति
teashop	*ciyā pasal*	चिया पसल
village	*gāū̃*	गाउँ

Do you have ...?	*tapāīsanga ... cha?*	तपाईंसंग ... छ ?
a bag	*jholā*	झोला
a carrybasket	**d**oko	डोको
firewood	*dāurā*	दाउरा
a knife	*cakku*	चक्कु
a Nepali knife	*khukuri*	खुकुरी
a stove	*stobh*	स्टोभ

What time are you ...?	*kati baje ...?*	कति बजे ... ?
getting up	*uthne*	उठ्ने
going to sleep	*sutna jāne*	सुत्न जाने

Weather

What's the weather like?
mausam kasto cha? मौसम कस्तो छ ?
The weather is ... today.
āja mausam ... cha आज मौसम ... छ

Will it be ...	*bholi mausam ...*	भोलि मौसम ...
tomorrow?	*holā?*	होला ?
bad/good	*kharāb/rāmro*	खराब / राम्रो
cloudy/foggy	*badali/kuhiro*	बदली / कुहिरो
cold/hot	*jādo/garmi*	जाडो / गर्मी
humid	*bāspiya*	बाष्पीय
rainy/sunny	*pāni parcha/ ghamāilo*	पानी पर्छ / घमाईलो
windy	*hāwādāri*	हावादारि

Some Useful Words

summer	*garmi mausam*	गर्मी मौसम
autumn	*sharad ritu*	शरद ऋतु
winter	*jādo mahinā*	जाडो महिना
spring	*basanta ritu*	बसन्त ऋतु
blizzard	*hiūko āndhi*	हिउँको आँधी
climate	*hāwāpāni*	हावापानी
cloud	*bādal*	बादल
earth/nature	*prithivi*	प्रिथिवी
frost	*tusāro*	तुसारो
ice	*baraph*	बरफ
lightning	*bijuli camkāi*	बिजुली चम्काई
monsoon	*barsā yukta*	बर्षायुक्त
mud	*hilo*	हिलो
rainbow	*indra dhanu*	इन्द्रधनु
rainy season	*barsā yām*	बर्षायाम
sky	*ākāsh*	आकाश
snow	*hiū*	हिउं

TREKKING

soil	*māto*	माटो
storm	*huri*	हुरी
sun	*surya*	सुर्य
thunder	*garjan*	गर्जन
thunderstorm	*megh garjan tathā barsā*	मेघगर्जन तथा बर्षा

Geographical Terms

agriculture	*khetipāti*	खेतीपाती
bridge	*pul*	पुल
cave	*guphā*	गुफा
creek	*kholā*	खोला
earthquake	*bhuincālo*	भुंईचालो
farm	*khetbāri*	खेतबारी
forest/jungle	*ban*	बन
hanging bridge	*jholunge pul*	झोलुङ्गे पुल
hill	*pahād*	पहाड
lake	*tāl*	ताल
landslide	*pahiro*	पहिरो

USEFUL TIP

Handy *'Hajur'*

You can use this word in many different situations. Say it: if you haven't heard or understood what someone's said to you; in addition to the answer of a simple 'Yes/No' question; or to express agreement or confirmation of what someone's said.

mountain/snow peak	*himāl*	हिमाल
pass	*bhanjyāng*	भन्ज्याङ्ग
peak	*cucuro*	चुचुरो
plains	*madesh/tarāi*	मदेश/तराई
pond	*pokhari*	पोखरी
river	*nadi*	नदी
scenery	*drishya*	द्रीश्य
trail	*sāno bāto*	सानो बाटो
waterfall	*jharanā*	झरना

Animals

bear	*bhālu*	भालु
buffalo	*bhainsi/rāngā*	भैंसी (f)/रांङ्गा (m)
camel	*ŭt*	ऊँट
cat	*birālo*	बिरालो
cow	*gāi*	गाई
crocodile	*gohi*	गोही
deer	*mriga*	म्रीग
dog	*kukur*	कुकुर
donkey	*gadhā*	गधा
elephant	*hātti*	हात्ती
fish	*māchā*	माछा
fox	*phyāuro*	प्याउरो
frog	*bhyāguto*	भ्यागुतो
goat	*bākhro*	बाख्रो
(castrated male)	*khasi*	खसी
horse	*ghodā*	घोडा
jackal	*syāl*	स्याल

leopard	*cituwā*	चितुवा
lion	*simha*	सिंह
lizard	*chepāro*	छेपारो
mole	*chucundro*	छुचुन्द्रो
mongoose	*nyāuri muso*	न्याउरी मूसो
monkey	*bāndar*	बाँदर
mouse/rat	*musā*	मूसा
ox	*goru*	गोरु
pet	*pāltu janāwar*	पाल्तु जनावर
pig	*sungur*	सुंगुर
rabbit	*kharāyo*	खरायो
rhinoceros	*gaĩdā*	गैंडा
sheep	*bhedā*	भेंडा
snake	*sarpa*	सर्प
squirrel	*lokharke*	लोखर्के
tiger	*bāgh*	बाघ
yak	*caũrigāi*	चौंरीगाई
yeti	*yati*	यति

Birds

chicken	*kukhurā*	कुखुरा
crane	*sāras*	सारस
crow	*kāg*	काग
dove	*dhukur*	धुकुर
duck	*hā̃s*	हाँस
eagle/kite	*cil*	चील
falcon	*bāj*	बाज
hen	*kukhuri*	कुखुरी

owl	*ullu*	उल्लु
parrot	*sugā*	सुगा
peacock	*mayur*	मयुर
pheasant	*kālij*	कालिज
pigeon	*parewā*	परेवा
rooster	*bhāle kukhurā*	भाले कुखुरा
vulture	*giddha*	गिद्ध

Insects

ant	*kamilā*	कमिला
bee	*māhuri*	माहुरी
butterfly	*putali*	पुतली
cockroach	*sānglo*	साँङ्लो
flea	*upiyā̃*	उपियाँ
fly	*jhingā*	झिंगा
leech/worm	*jukā*	जुका
louse	*jumrā*	जुम्रा
mosquito	*lāmkhutte*	लामखुट्टे
scorpion	*bicchi*	बिच्छी
snail	*sankha kirā*	शंखकीरा
spider	*mākurā*	माकुरा
tick	*kirno*	किर्नो

TREKKING

USEFUL TIP

Don't overdo it!

'Please' and 'Thank you' are not used in Nepali as much as they are in English.

Plants

branch	*hāngā*	हाँगा
bush	*jhādi*	झाडी
flower	*phul*	फूल
leaf	*pāt*	पात
poinsettia	*lāli pāte*	लालिपाते
rhododendron	*lāli gurāns*	लालिगुराँस
stick	*latthi*	लट्ठी
sugar cane	*ukhu*	उखु
tree	*rukh*	रुख
wood	*kāth*	काठ

Some Useful Phrases

Am I allowed to camp here?
   yahā̃ shivir garna huncha?   यहाँ शिविर गर्नहुन्छ ?

Is there a campsite nearby?
   ke tyahā̃ shivir najik cha?   के त्यहाँ शिविर नजिक छ ?

I want to hire (a) ...	*malāi ... bhādāmā cāhiyo*	मलाई ... भाँडामा चाहियो
backpack	*jholā*	झोला
sleeping bag	*sutne jholā*	सुल्ने झोला
stove	*stobh*	स्टोभ
tent	*pāl*	पाल

Can I get there on foot?
tyahā̃ hĩdera jāna sakcha? त्यहाँ हिंडेर जान सक्छ ?

Do I need a guide?
bāto dekhāunu parcha? बाटो देखाउनुपर्छ ?

Can I swim here?
yahā̃ paudi khelna sakchu? यहाँ पौडि खेल्न सक्छु ?

What's that animal/plant called?
tyo janāwar/biruwā lāi ke bhancha? त्यो जनावर/बिरुवा लाई के भन्छ ?

I want to look at your trekking permit.
tapāīko anumati patra hernu parcha तपाईंको अनुमती पत्र हर्नुपर्छ

Are you going by yourself?
tapāī āphai jāne? तपाईं आफै जाने ?

I have to rest.
malāi ārām linu parcha मलाई आराम लिनुपर्छ

Let's sit in the shade.
shitalmā basaũ शितलमा बकौं

Carry me slowly.
malāi bistārai boknuhos मलाई बिस्तारै बोक्नुहोस

I have to urinate/defecate.
malāi pisāb/disā lāgyo मलाई पिसाब/दिसा लाग्यो

Some Useful Words

easy	*sajilo*	सजिलो
far	*tādhā*	टाढा
fast	*chito/cādai*	छिटो/चाँडै
heavy	*gahraũ*	गह्रौ
hill (person)	*pahādi*	पहाडि
kerosene	*mati tel*	मटितेल
lamp/light	*batti*	बत्ती
mountaineer	*parbatārohi*	पर्वतारोही
OK/Alright.	*thik cha*	ठीक छ
plainsdweller	*madeshi*	मदेशी
shelter	*bās*	बास
slow/late	*dhilo*	ढिलो
small	*sāno*	सानो
stone	*dhungā*	ढुङ्गा
(to) trek	*paidal yātrā (garnu)*	पैदल यात्रा गर्नु
to walk	*hĩdnu*	हिंड्नु

TREKKING

Food

In the restaurants of Kathmandu and other large towns, all kinds of dishes are available, including a wide range of Western-style food. But in the country, and on trekking routes, food is much simpler, and at any one time of the year only a few different food items are available.

The most typical Nepali meal is *dāl bhāt tarakāri*: boiled rice with lentils and vegetable curry. It is usually served with a fresh pickle or relish which may be very spicy. In the hills, potatoes, corn, millet and other carbohydrates are also staple foods. Meat is scarce and expensive, and tends to be served mainly on festival days and other special occasions. Remember that in Hindu Nepal cows are sacred and beef is not eaten. This means that vegetarian meals are widely available. The meat likely to be available is buff (water buffalo), goat, chicken or even yak.

In Nepal two meals a day are the norm, one around 10 or 11 am and the second at 7 or 8 pm, with just a glass of tea after getting up. In less touristy areas, you may not be able to get any food before 10 am.

When invited into a private home, always remove your shoes, leaving them outside the door or where everyone else leaves theirs.

FOOD

102

Hindus, particularly those of high caste, do not usually eat in company, and it is a great honour to be asked to share a meal. Buddhists, as most hillpeople, don't place much emphasis on privacy. If you share a meal, you will probably sit on a mat on the floor, with your legs crossed, and eat off a dish placed on the floor. Remember to always use your right hand for eating. You can use your left hand to hold a glass. It is important to wash or rinse your hand and mouth before sitting down and again after eating. Food or drink from your own plate or cup cannot be shared with anyone else, so don't take more than you can eat. This can be difficult to put into practice, as you will be treated as an honoured guest, and your plate will often be refilled without your asking.

breakfast	*bihānako khānā*	बिहानको खाना
lunch	*camenā*	चमेना
dinner/food/meal	*bhāt*	भात
restaurant	*bhojanālaya*	भोजनालय
snack	*khājā*	खाजा
teashop	*ciyā pasal*	चिया पसल
(to) drink	*piunu*	पिउनु
(to) eat	*khānu*	खानु

The verb *khānu* is commonly used for drinking and smoking:

I eat rice.
  ma bhāt khānchu म भात खान्छु

I drink tea.
  ma ciyā khānchu म चिया खान्छु

I don't smoke cigarettes.
  ma curot khāndina म चुरोट खान्दिन

At the Restaurant

Waiter!

dāju! (man)	दाजु !	
bhāi! (boy)	भाइ !	
didi! (woman)	दिदी !	
bahini! (girl)	बहिनी !	

Please show me the menu.
menu dinuhos
मेनु दिनुहोस

Can I have a little ...?   *alikati ... dinuhos*   अलिकति ... दिनुहोस

drinking water	*khāne pāni*	खाने पानी
rice	*bhāt*	भात
soup	*jhol*	झोल

Please give me ...   *malāi ... dinuhos*   मलाई ... दिनुहोस

cold beer	*ciso biyar*	चिसो बियर
a meal	*khānā*	खाना

I can't eat spicy food.
ma piro khāna sakdina
म पिरो खान सक्दिन

What is this/that?
yo/tyo ke ho?
यो / त्यो के हो ?

I'm hungry/thirsty.
malāi bhok/tirkhā lāgyo
मलाई भोक / तिर्खा लाग्यो

The meal was delicious.
khānā mitho lāgyo
खाना मिठो लाग्यो

The food isn't hot.
  khānā tāto chaina　　खाना तातो छैन
Please bring me ...
  malāi ... lyāunuhos　　मलाई ... ल्याउनुहोस्

Vegetarian

I'm a vegetarian.
  ma sākāhāri hū̃　　म साकाहारी हुँ

I don't eat ...	*ma ... khāndina*	म ... खान्दिन
meat	*māsu*	मासु
fish	*māchā*	माछा
dairy products	*dugdha shālāko khānā*	दूधशालाको खाना

Table Articles

cup	*kap*	कप
dishes/utensils	*bhā̃dā kū̃dā*	भाँडाकुँडा
fork	*kāntā*	काँटा
glass	*gilās*	गिलास
jug	*surāhi*	सुराहि
knife	*cakku*	चक्क
napkin/towel	*rumāl*	रुमाल
plate	*thāl*	थाल
spoon	*camcā*	चम्चा
toothpick	*sinko*	सिन्को
a cup of ...	*ek kap ...*	एक कप ...
a glass of ...	*ek gilās ...*	एक गिलास ...
a packet of ...	*ek poko ...*	एक पोको ...

At the Market

How much per kg?
ek kiloko kati parcha?
एक किलोको कति पर्छ ?

That's all, how much is it?
teti mātrai, kati bhayo?
तेति मात्रै, कति भयो ?

Where is the weekly market?
hāt bajār kahā̃ cha?
हात बजार कहाँ छ ?

When is the weekly market?
hāt bajār kahile huncha?
हात बजार कहिले हुन्छ ?

Meat

English	Romanised	Devanagari
buff (water buffalo)	*rāngāko māsu*	राँगाको मासु
chicken	*kukhurāko māsu*	कुखुराको मासु
(dried) fish	*(sukeko) māchā*	(सुकेको) माछा
eel	*bām*	बाम
egg	*phul/andā*	फुल / अण्डा
goat	*khasiko māsu*	खसीको मासु
liver	*kalejoko māsu*	कलेजोको मासु
meat	*māsu*	मासु
dried meat	*sukuti*	सुकुति
pork	*sungurko māsu*	सुँगुरको मासु
yak meat	*caũrigāiko māsu*	चौंरीगाईको मासु

FOOD

Vegetables

green beans	*simi*	सिमी
cabbage	*bandā kobi*	बन्दाकोबि
carrot	*gājar*	गाजर
cauliflower	*kāuli*	काउली
chilli pepper	*khursāni*	खुर्सानी
choko squash	*iskus*	ईस्कुस
corn	*makai*	मकै
cucumber	*kānkro*	काँक्रो
dried vegetable	*gundruk*	गुन्द्रुक
eggplant (long)	*bhāntā*	भाण्टा
(ovoid)	*brinjal*	ब्रीन्जल
garlic	*lasun*	लसुन
green pepper	*bhẽdā khursāni*	भेंडा खुर्सानी
leafy vegetables	*sāg pāt*	सागपात
lettuce	*jiriko sāg*	जिरीको साग
mushroom	*cyāu*	च्याउ
mustard greens	*rāyoko sāg*	रायोको साग
onion	*pyāj*	प्याज
parsley	*jwānoko sāg*	ज्वानोको साग
peas	*kerāu*	केराउ
popcorn	*bhuteko makai*	भुटेको मकै
potato	*ālu*	आलु
pumpkin	*pharsi*	फर्सि
radish	*mulā*	मुला
spinach	*pālungo*	पालुङ्गे
squash		
(bitter gourd)	*karelo*	करेलो
(long green)	*laukā*	लौका

FOOD

sweet potato	*sakhar khanda*	सखर खण्ड
tomato	*golbhēdā*	गोलभेंडा
turnip	*salgam*	सल्गम
vegetables	*tarakāri*	तरकारी
yam	*tarul*	तरुल
zucchini	*ghiraunlo*	घिरौलो

Dairy Products

butter	*makhan*	मखन
cheese	*cij*	चीज
cream	*tar*	तर
ghee	*ghiu*	घिउ
ice cream	*khuwā baraph*	खुवा बरफ
milk	*dudh*	दूध
yak milk	*caūrigāiko dudh*	चौरीगाईको दूध
yoghurt (curd)	*dahi*	दहि

Where was this cheese made?
   yo cij kahā̃ baneko ho?   यो चीज कहाँ बनेको हो ?
What kind of milk is it made
from?
   kun dudh bāta baneko ho?   कुन दूधबाट बनेको हो ?
Where can you get this kind
of cheese?
   yasto cij kahā̃ pāincha?   यस्तो चीज कहाँ पाईन्छ ?

Fruit

apple	syāu	स्याउ
apricot	khurapāni	खुरपानी
banana	kerā	केरा
cherry	paiyunkhālko phal	पैयूँखालको फल
coconut	nariwal	नरिवल
dates	choharā	छोहरा
fig	anjir	अन्जीर
fruit	phalphul	फलफूल
grape	angur	अँगुर
grapefruit	bhogate	भोगटे
guava	ambā	अम्बा
lemon/lime	kāgati	कागती
lychee	lici	लीची
mandarin/orange	suntalā	सुन्तला
mango	āmp	आँप
melon	tarbujā	तर्बुजा
papaya	mewā	मेवा
peach	āru	आरु
pear	nāspāti	नास्पाती
pineapple	bhuĩ katahar	भुईंकटहर
plum	āru bakhadā	आरु बखडा
pomegranate	anār	अनार
raisin	dākh	दाख
sweet lime	musam	मुसम

Cereals & Legumes

barley/oats	*jau*	जौउ
lentils (black)	*kālo dāl*	कालो दाल
(brown)	*khairo dāl*	खैरो दाल
(red)	*musur dāl*	मुसुर दाल
millet	*kodo*	कोदो
rice (unhusked)	*dhān*	धान
(uncooked)	*cāmal*	चामल
(cooked)	*bhāt*	भात
soybeans	*bhatmās*	भटमास
wheat	*gahū*	गहुँ

Bread

biscuit/cookie	*biskut*	बिस्कुट
bread	*roti*	रोटी
(flat)	*capāti*	चपाटी
(flat, deep fried)	*puri*	पुरि
(loaf)	*pāu roti*	पाउरोटी
flour	*pitho*	पीठो

Nuts

almond	*kāgati badām*	कागटी बदाम
cashew	*kāju*	काजु
nuts	*supāri*	सुपारी
peanut	*badām*	बदाम
walnut	*okhar*	ओखर

Herbs, Spices & Condiments

basil	*tulasi*	तुलसी
cardamom	*sukmel*	सुकमेल
chilli pepper	*khursāni*	खुर्सानी
cinnamon	*dālcini*	दालचिनी
cloves	*lwāng*	ल्वाङ्ग
coriander	*dhaniyã*	धनियाँ
(fresh)	*hariyo dhaniyã*	हरीयो धनियाँ
cumin	*jirā*	जीरा
fennel	*soph*	सोफ
fenugreek	*methi*	मेठी
ginger	*aduwā*	अदुवा
honey	*maha*	मह
mustard (oil)	*toriko tel*	तोरीको तेल
(seed)	*toriko biu*	तोरीको बिउ
nutmeg	*jāiphal*	जाईफल
oil	*tel*	तेल
pepper(corn)	*maric*	मरिच
pickle/relish	*acār*	अचार
saffron	*keshar*	केशर
salt	*nun*	नुन
sesame seeds	*tilko biu*	तिलको बिउ
sugar	*cini*	चिनी
sugar cane	*ukhu*	उखु
tamarind/sour fruit	*amili*	अमिलि
turmeric	*besār*	बेसार
vinegar	*sirkā*	सिर्खा

Drinks

alcohol	*raksi*	रक्सी
beer	*biyar*	बियर
(millet)	*tumbā*	तूम्बा
(rice)	*chayāng*	छयाङ्ग
black coffee	*kālo kaphi*	कालो कफी
juice	*ras*	रस
lemon tea	*kāgati ciyā*	कागती चिया
milk tea	*ciyā*	चिया
milk coffee	*dudh kaphi*	दूध कफी
water	*pāni*	पानी
boiled water	*umāleko pāni*	उमालेको पानी

USEFUL TIP

To answer a question you don't use 'Yes' or 'No'. Just repeat the verb in the question in the affirmative or negative.

Some Useful Phrases

Do you like beer?
tapāīlāi biyar man parcha?   तपाईंलाई बियर मनपर्छ ?

Yes/No.
man parcha/man pardaina   मनपर्छ / मनपर्दैन

What would you like?
tapāīlāi ke man paryo?   तपाईंलाई के मनपर्यो ?

Would you like tea or coffee?
tapāīlāi ciyā ki kaphi?   तपाईंलाई चिया कि कफी ?

I'd like coffee.
malāi kaphi   मलाई कफी

Some Useful Words

bitter	*tito*	तीतो
cold	*ciso*	चिसो
contaminated	*jhuto*	झूटो
(to) cook	*pakāunu*	पकाउनु
delicious	*mitho*	मिठो
empty	*khāli*	खाली
(to) feed	*khuwāunu*	खुवाउनु
fresh	*tājā*	ताजा
fried	*bhuteko*	भुटेको
hot (spicy)	*piro*	पिरो
(temperature)	*tāto*	तातो
kitchen	*bhānchā*	भान्छा
raw/unripe	*kānco*	काँचो
ripe/cooked	*pākeko*	पाकेको

FOOD

salty	*nunilo*	नुनिलो
sour	*amilo*	अमीलो
spicy	*piro*	पिरो
stale/leftover	*bāsi*	बासी
sweet	*guliyo*	गुलियो

Shopping

In Kathmandu and other towns, most shopkeepers speak some English, but outside the more populated areas this is not necessarily the case. Remember, there is a special form of address for proprietors of shops, restaurants, hotels or guesthouses. (See Greetings & Civilities, page 39.)

They may respond with *bhannuhos* ('speak'). Remember that 'Please' and 'Thank you' are not necessary. Just state what you want and add *dinuhos* ('Please give'). Generally, bargaining is not appropriate for basic household goods or foodstuffs (except fruit which is a luxury).

Nepali currency is the rupee *(rupaiyā)*. It is divided into 100 *paisā*, which is also the word for 'money'.

Where is the nearest ...?	*najikai ... kahā̃ cha?*	नजिकै ... कहाँ छ ?
bank	*baink*	बैंक
barber	*hajām*	हजाम
bookshop	*kitāb pasal*	किताब पसल
chemist/pharmacy	*ausadhi pasal*	औषधी पसल
clothing store	*lugā pasal*	लुगा पसल

115

cobbler	*sārki*	सार्की
laundry	*lugā dhune thāū*	लुगाधुने ठाउँ
market	*bajār*	बजार
shoeshop	*juttā pasal*	जुत्ता पसल
teashop	*ciyā pasal*	चिया पसल
vegetable shop	*tarakāri pasal*	तरकारी पसल

I'd like to buy a ...
  ... *kinna man lāgyo*   ... किन्न मनलाग्यो
I'm just looking.
  herdaichu   हेर्दैछु
How much is this pen?
  yo kalamko kati paisā ho?   यो कलमको कति पैसा हो ?
How much do eggs cost?
  phulko kati ho?   फुलको कति हो ?
Four rupees each.
  eutāko cār rupaiyā̃   एउटाको चार रुपैयाँ

Where can I	... *kahā̃ kinna*	... कहाँ किन्न
buy ...?	*pāincha?*	पाइन्छ ?
paper	*kāgaj*	कागज
soap	*sābun*	साबुन
string	*dori*	डोरी

Do you have a ...?	*tapāīkahā̃ cha?*	तपाईकहाँ ... छ ?
cap	*topi*	टोपी
newspaper	*akhabār*	अखबार
pencil	*sisā kalam*	सिसाकलम

Bargaining

In Nepal it is customary to bargain *(moltol garnu)*, especially for tourist and luxury goods and transport. As in most other Asian countries, friendly bargaining is a way of life, and foreigners are (realistically) presumed wealthier than locals. But there will be a going price for ordinary goods, such as foodstuffs.

Tibet is one of the few places where bargaining is not the norm, but this attitude changes dramatically when Tibetans trade in Nepal!

Do you have Tibetan dresses?
   tapāīkahā̃ cubā cha?

तपाईकहाँ चुबा छ ?

Yes, have a look.
   cha, hernuhos

छ, हेर्नुहोस

How much is this one?
   yasko kati parcha?

यस्को कति पर्छ ?

Three hundred rupees.
   tin say rupaiyā̃

तीनशय रुपैयाँ

That's expensive.
   mahango bhayo

महँगो भयो

It's cheap!
   sasto cha!

सस्तो छ !

I don't have that much money.
   masanga teti paisā chaina

मसंग तेती पैसा छैन

Could you lower the price?
> *alikati ghatāunu huncha ki?* अलिकति घटाउनुहुन्छ कि ?

I'll give you 200 rupees.
> *ma dui say rupaiyā̃ dinchu* म दुईशय रुपैयाँ दिन्छु

That's not possible, give me 250.
> *hundaina, dui say pacās* हुन्दैन, दुईशय पचास
> *dinuhos* दिनुहोस्

OK.
> *huncha* हुनछ

No, I don't want it.
> *cāhindaina* चाहिन्दैन

Souvenirs

anklet	*pāuju*	पाउजु
bangle	*curā*	चुरा
brassware	*pitalko sāmān*	पितलको सामान
carpet	*galaincā*	गलैंचा
chain	*sikri*	सिक्री
(a pair of) earrings	*ek jor tap*	एक जोर टप
embroidery	*buttā*	बुट्टा
gem/jewel	*juhārāt*	जुहारात
gold	*sun*	सुन
handicraft	*hastakalā*	हस्तकला
incense burner	*dhup dāni*	धूप दानि
jewellery/ornament	*gahanā*	गहना
mask	*makundo*	मकुण्डो
necklace	*mālā*	माला
Nepali knife	*khukuri*	खुकुरी

painting	citra/thāngkā	चित्र / थाङ्का
pottery	mātoko sāmān	माटोको सामान
ring	aunthi	औंठी
silver	cāndi	चाँदी
statue	murti	मूर्ति
souvenirs	cino	चिनो
wooden article	kāth bāta baneko bastu	काठबाट बैको वस्तु

Clothing

Nepali national dress is a sari *(sādi)* and blouse *(colo)* for women, and a tunic *(dāurā)* and trousers *(suruwāl)* for men.

Can I try it on?
　lagāi herna huncha? लगाई हेर्नहुन्छ ?

Can you make one for me?
　malāi eutā lugā banāi मलाई एउटा लुगा बनाईदिनु
　dinu sakincha? सकिन्छ ?

It fits well/doesn't fit.
　thik cha/chaina ठीक छ / छैन

It's too ...	dherai ... cha	धेरै ... छ
big/small	thulo/sāno	ठूलो / सानो
short/long	choto/lāmo	छोटो / लामो
tight/loose	kasincha/khukulo	कसिन्छ / खुकुलो

belt	peti	पेटी
button	tānk	टाँक
cap/hat	topi	टोपी
cloth	kapadā	कपडा
clothing	lugāharu	लुगाहरु
coat	kot	कोट्
dress/frock	jāmā	जामा
gloves	panjā	पञ्जा
to get dressed	lugā lagāunu	लुगा लगाउनु
muffler	galbandi	गलबनदी
scarf	dopattā	दोपट्टा
shirt	kamij	कमिज
shoes	juttā	जुत्ता
socks	mojā	मोजा
sandals	cappal	चप्पल
shorts/underpants	kattu	कट्टु
T-shirt/singlet	ganji	गन्जी
vest/waistcoat	istakot	ईस्टकोट्

Materials

| cotton | suti | सुति |
| handmade | hātle baneko | हातले बनेको |

leather	*chālā*	छाला
silk	*resham*	रेशम
wool	*un*	उन

Colours

black	*kālo*	कालो
blue	*nilo*	निलो
bright	*ujyālo*	उज्यालो
brown	*khairo*	खैरो
dark	*andhyāro*	अँध्यारो
green	*hariyo*	हरियो
light	*ujyālo*	उज्यालो
multicoloured	*rangin*	रंङ्गीन
orange	*suntalā rang*	सुन्तलारङ्ग
pale	*phikkā*	फिक्का
pink	*gulāphi*	गुलाफि
purple	*pyāji*	प्याजि
red	*rāto*	रातो
white	*seto*	सेतो
yellow	*pahēlo*	पहेँलो

USEFUL TIP

Manners!
Remember to use the particular term of address for
proprietors of shops, restaurants, hotels and guesthouses. (See page 39)

Toiletries

comb	*kāīyo*	काईयो
condom	*dhāl*	ढाल
hairbrush	*kapāl korne burus*	कपाल कोर्ने बुरुस
laxative	*julāph*	जुलाफ
razorblade	*patti*	पत्ती
shampoo	*dhulāi*	धुलाई
soap	*sābun*	साबुन
toilet paper	*twāilet pepar*	टवाईलेट् पेपर
toothbrush	*dānt mājhne burus*	दाँत माझ्ने बुरुस
toothpaste	*manjan*	मञ्जन

Stationery & Publications

aerogram	*hawāi patra*	हवाईपत्र
airmail	*hawāi dāk*	हवाईडाक
book	*kitāb*	किताब
dictionary	*shabda kosh*	शब्दकोश
envelope	*khām*	खाम
exercise book/ notebook	*kāpi*	कापि
ink	*masi*	मसि
letterpad	*citthi lekhne kāpi*	चिठ्ठीलेख्ने कापि
magazine	*patra patrikā*	पत्रपत्रीका
map	*naksā*	नक्सा
newspaper	*akhabār*	अखबार
novel	*upanyās*	उपन्यास
paper	*kāgaj*	कागज
pen	*kalam*	कलम

pencil	*sisā kalam*	सिसाकलम
scissors	*kainci*	कैंची
stamp	*tikat*	टिकट
writing pad	*lekhne kāpi*	लेखने कापि

Photography

Please give me a film for this camera.

yo kyāmerālāi euta ril dinuhos
यो क्यामेरालाई एउटा रील दिनुहोस

How much is it for developing?

euta ril print garna, kati paisā lāgcha?
एउटा रील प्रिन्ट गर्न, कति पैसा लाग्छ ?

When will it be ready?

kahile āune?
कहिले आउने ?

Do you fix cameras?

kyāmerā banāunu huncha?
क्यामेरा बनाउनुहुन्छ ?

| colour film | *rangin ril* | रंङीन रील |
| B&W film | *kālo seto ril* | कालो सेतो रील |

Smoking

| cigarette | *curot* | चुरोट |
| hashish | *cares* | चरेस |

hemp	*bhāng*	भाङ्ग
hookah	*hukkā*	हुक्का
marijuana	*gānjā*	गाँजा
matches	*salāi*	सलाई
pipe	*curot pāip*	चुरोट पाईप्
tobacco	*surti*	सुर्ती

Do you have a light?
    salāi cha?   सलाई छ ?
A packet of cigarettes, please.
    ek battā curot dinuhos   एक बट्टा चुरोट् दिनुहोस

Weights & Measures

The metric system is in common use, but there are some measures particular to Nepal:

kg/litre	*mānā*	माना
handful	*muthi*	मुथि
200 grams	*pāu*	पाउ
800 grams	*ser*	सेर
metre	*gaj*	गज
span	*bitto*	बित्तो

Size & Quantity

enough	*prashasta*	प्रशस्त
heavy	*gahraũ*	गह्रौँ
less	*ajha kamti*	अझ कम्ती

light (weight)	*halukā*	हलुका
a little (bit)	*ali kati*	अलि कति
long	*lāmo*	लामो
(too) many/much	*dherai*	धेरै
more	*ajha dherai*	अझ धेरै
some/any	*kehi, kunai*	केहि, कुनै
tall	*aglo*	अग्लो
too	*sāhrai*	साह्रै

Some Useful Phrases

I would like to buy ...
   malāi ... kinna man lāgyo   मलाई ... किन्न मनलाग्यो

Do you have others?
   arko kunai cha?   अर्को कुनै छ ?

May I see it?
   heraū   हेरैं

I like/don't like (this).
   malāi man parcha/man pardaina   मलाई मनपर्छ / मनपर्दैन

I'll take it.
   linchu   लिन्छु

There is none.
   chaina   छैन

Which one?
   kun cāhī?   कुन चाहियो ?

This one?
   yo?   यो ?

Please show it (to me).
  dekhāunuhos

देखाउनुहोस

Please show (me) the price.
  mol dekhāunuhos

मोल देखाउनुहोस

What is it made of?
  kele baneko?

केले बनेको ?

Where was it made?
  kahā̃ baneko?

कहाँ बनेको ?

What else do you need?
  aru kehi cāhincha ki?

अरु केहि चाहिन्छ कि ?

That's all, how much is it?
  teti mātrai, kati bhayo?

तेति मात्रै, कति भयो ?

Do you accept credit cards?
  kredit kard huncha?

क्रेडीटकर्ड हुन्छ ?

Is your carpet old or new?
  *tapāīko galaincā nayā̃ ho
  ki purāno?*

तपाईंको गलैंचा नयाँ हो
कि पुरानो ?

Where is the weekly market?
  hāt bajār kahā̃ cha?

हात बजार कहाँ छ ?

When is the weekly market?
  hāt bajār kahile huncha?

हात बजार कहिले हुन्छ ?

Some Useful Words

(is) available	*pāincha*	पाईन्छ
bag/pack	*jholā*	झोला
basket	*tokari*	टोकरि
battery	*masalā*	मसला
bottle	*sisi*	सिसी
box	*bākas*	बाकस
bucket	*bāltin*	बाल्टीन
buy (v)	*kinnu*	किन्नु
carrybasket	*doko*	डोको
cheap	*sasto*	सस्तो
expensive	*mahango*	महँगो
mat	*gundari*	गुन्दरि
mirror	*ainā*	ऐना
needle	*siyo*	सियो
new	*nayā̃*	नयाँ
old	*purāno*	पुरानो
packet	*poko/battā*	पोको / बट्टा
receipt/bill	*bil*	बिल
to repair	*marmat garnu*	मर्मत गर्नु
shop (n)	*pasal*	पसल

spend	*kharca garnu*	खर्च गर्नु
string/rope	*dori*	डोरि
thread	*dhāgo*	धागो
total	*jammā*	जम्मा
umbrella	*chātā*	छाता

Health

Never drink tap or river water unless it has been boiled and preferably also filtered. Bottled water is widely available and quite cheap. Nepali pharmacies stock a wide range of Western medicines, available without prescription, and they can give helpful advice. Traditional Ayurvedic medicines from plants are also prepared in Nepal. Tibetan medicines are another alternative.

I'm sick.
ma birāmi chu — म बिरामि छु

I need to be seen by a doctor.
*malāi **dā**ktar jancāunu paryo* — मलाई डाक्टर जँचाउनुपर्यो

Where can I find a good doctor?
*rāmro **dā**ktar kaha pāincha?* — राम्रो डाक्टर कहाँ पाईन्छ ?

Please call a doctor.
dāktarlāi bolāunuhos — डाक्टरलाई बोलाउनुहोस

Where is a/the ...?	... *kahā̃ cha?*	... कहाँ छ ?
chemist/pharmacy	*ausadhi pasal*	औषधी पसल
dentist	*dāntko **dā**ktar*	दाँतको डाक्टर
health post/clinic	*cikitsālaya*	चिकित्सालय
hospital	*aspatāl*	अस्पताल

HEALTH

Where is the nearest hospital?
   najikai aspatāl kahā̃ cha?   नजिकै अस्पताल कहाँ छ ?
I need a porter.
   malāi bhariyā cāhiyo   मलाइ भरिया चाहियो
Please carry me to ...
   ... samma malāī boknuhos   ... सम्म मलाई बोक्नुहोस
Please send a message.
   khabar pathāunuhos   खबर पठाउनुहोस

Complaints

My ... hurts	*mero ... dukhyo*	मेरो ... दुख्यो
eye	*ānkhā*	आँखा
head	*tāuko*	टाउको
stomach	*pet*	पेट
tooth	*dānt*	दाँत

He/She broke	*wahā̃ko ...*	वहाँको ...
his/her ...	*bhāncyo*	भाँच्यो
ankle	*goli gāntho*	गोलि गाँठो
arm	*pākhurā*	पाखुरा
leg	*khuttā*	खुट्टा

It hurts here.
   yahā̃ dukhyo   यहाँ दुख्यो
I feel dizzy/weak.
   malāī ringatā/kamjor lāgyo   मलाई रिंगटा/कमजोर लाग्यो ।
I have a headache.
   mero kapāl dukhyo   मेरो कपाल दुख्यो

HEALTH

I've been bitten.
   malāi tokyo — मलाई टोक्यो

I burned my ...
   mero ... mā polyo — मेरो ...मा पोल्यो

I'm having trouble breathing.
   sās pherna sakdina — सास फेर्न सक्दिन

I've vomited.
   bāntā garē — बान्ता गरें

I can't sleep.
   sutna sakdina — सुत्न सक्दिन

I can't move my ...
   mero ... calāuna sakdina — मेरो ... चलाउन सक्दिन

I have ...	*malāi ... lāgyo*	मलाई ... लाग्यो
altitude sickness	*uccāi*	उच्चाइ
arthritis/rheumatism	*bath*	बाथ
asthma	*damko byathā*	दमको ब्यथा
bronchitis	*swās naliko rog*	स्वास नलीको रोग
cholera	*haijā*	हैजा
a cold	*rughā*	रुघा
constipation	*disā banda*	दिसा बन्द
a cough	*khoki*	खोकी
cramp	*baundyāi*	बौंडचाइ
a cut/wound	*ghāu*	घाउ
dehydration	*pāni sukāuna*	पानी सुकाउन
diabetes	*madhu meha*	मधुमेह
diarrhoea	*jhādā*	झाडा
dysentery	*ragat māsi*	रगतमासी

HEALTH

epilepsy	*chāre rog*	छारे रोग
fever	*jwaro*	ज्वरो
food poisoning	*khānā kharāb*	खाना खराब
frostbite	*tusārole khāyeko*	तुसारोले खायेको
indigestion	*apac*	अपच
an infection	*rog sarna*	रोग सर्न
an inflammation	*sunniyeko abasthā*	सुन्नीयेको अवस्था
influenza	*rughā khokiko jwaro*	रुघाखोकीको ज्वरो
an itch	*cilāuna*	चिलाउन
jaundice	*kamalpitta*	कमलपित्त
malaria	*aulo*	औलो
meningitis	*gidiko jālo sunnine rog*	गिदिको जालो सुन्नीने रोग
a pain	*dukhāi*	दुखाई
paralysis	*pachavāt*	पक्षवात
a rash	*rātopan*	रातोपन
a sore throat	*ghānti dukheko*	घाँटी दुखेको
a sprain	*markāi*	मर्काइ
sunstroke	*lu/ātapāghāt*	लु/आतपाघात
tuberculosis	*chaya rog*	क्षयरोग
typhoid	*tāiphāid*	टाइफाइड
venereal disease (syphillis)	*bhiringi*	भिरिंगि
worms	*jukā*	जुका

HEALTH

Women's Health

I'd like to see a female doctor.
malāi keti dāktar cāhiyo — मलाई केटी डक्टर चाहियो

I have a cramp.
malāi baundyāi lāgyo — मलाई बौंडचाइ लाग्यो

I haven't menstruated for ...
rajaswalā bhaye chaina ... samma — रजस्वला भये छैन ... सम्म

I'm (... weeks) pregnant.
ma garbhavati chu (... haptā bhayo) — म गर्भवती छु (... हप्ता भयो)

I'm taking the contraceptive pill.
ma garbhanirodhko ausadhi lindaichu — म गर्भनीरोधको औषधी लिन्दैछु

Allergies

I'm allergic to ... *malāi ... linu hundaina* — मलाई ... लिनुहुन्दैन

aspirin *āispirin* — आईसपिरिन्

that medicine *tyo ausadhi* — त्यो औषधी

The Doctor Might Say

Are you well?
tapāīlāi sancai cha? — तपाईलाई सञ्चै छ ?

What's the matter?
ke bhayo? — के भयो ?

When did your headache
start?
    kahile dekhi kapāl dukheko?   कहिले देखी कपाल दुखेको ?
Have you eaten?
    khānā khānu bhayo?   खाना खानु भयो ?
Did you take any medicine?
    ausadhi khānu bhayo?   औषधी खानु भयो ?

Parts of the Body

ankle	*goli gāntho*	गोलीगाँठो
appendix	*parishista*	परिशिष्ट
arm	*pākhurā*	पाखुरा
back	*pithū*	पिठुँ
backbone/spine	*dhād*	ढाड
brain	*gidi*	गिदि
breast	*stan*	स्तन
buttock	*cānk*	चाँक
chest	*chāti*	छाती
elbow	*kuhino*	कुहिनो
finger	*aunlā*	औंला
head	*tāuko*	टाउको
heart	*mutu*	मुटु
hip	*nitamba*	नितम्ब
joint	*jorni*	जोर्नी
kidney	*mrigaulā*	म्रिगौला
liver	*kalejo*	कलेजो

HEALTH

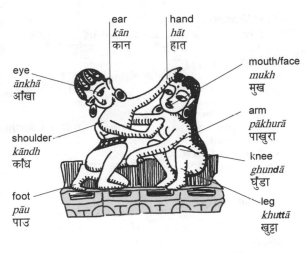

eye
ānkhā
आँखा

ear
kān
कान

hand
hāt
हात

mouth/face
mukh
मुख

arm
pākhurā
पाखुरा

shoulder
kāndh
काँध

knee
ghundā
घुंडा

foot
pāu
पाउ

leg
khuttā
खुट्टा

muscle	*māmshapeshi*	मांशपेशी
neck/throat	*ghānti*	घाँटी
nose	*nāk*	नाक
skin	*chālā*	छाला
stomach	*pet*	पेट
teeth/tooth	*dānt*	दाँत
tongue	*jibhro*	जिभ्रो
womb/uterus	*pāthe ghar*	पाठेघर
wrist	*nādi*	नाडि

HEALTH

At the Chemist

Please give me ...	*malāi ... dinuhos*	मलाई ... दिनुहोस
aspirin	*āisprin*	आईसपिरिन्
bandages	*patti*	पट्टी
iodine	*āidin*	आईडीन्
medicine	*ausadhi*	औषधी

I need something for ...
malāi ... lāgyo, kunai   मलाई ... लाग्यो, कुनै औषधी
ausadhi dinuhos   दिनुहोस
How many times a day?
dinko kati patak?   दिनको कति पटक ?

Some Useful Phrases

I have ...	*malāi ... lāgyo*	मलाई ... लाग्यो
asthma	*damko byathā*	दमको ब्यथा
diabetes	*madhu meha*	मधुमेह
epilepsy	*chāre rog*	छारे रोग

USEFUL TIP

Politely correct!
When addressing someone by name, it's
polite to add the word '*-ji*' to the end of
their name.

HEALTH

Is there a good dentist (here)?
rāmro dāntko dāktar cha? राम्रो दाँतको डक्टर छ ?

I have a toothache.
mero dānt dukheko cha मेरो दाँत दुखेको छ

Please give me an anaesthetic.
nishcetak dinuhos निश्चेतक दिनुहोस

I've been vaccinated.
sui lisakē सूई लिसकें

I have my own syringe/needle.
masanga āphno siyo cha मसंग आफ्नो सियो छ

I'm feeling OK now.
ahile thik bhayo अहिले ठीक भयो

Some Useful Words

accident	*durghatanā*	दुर्घटना
ache (v)	*dukhnu*	दुख्नु
addiction/habit	*lat/bāni*	लत / बानी
bleed	*ragat āunu*	रगत आउनु
blood pressure	*rakta cāp*	रक्तचाप
contraception	*garbhanirodh*	गर्भनिरोध
disease/illness	*rog*	रोग
injection	*sui*	सूई
injury	*cot patak*	चोट पटक
itch	*cilcilāhat*	चिलचिलाहट
menstruation	*rajaswalā*	रजस्वला
nausea	*wākwāki*	वाकवाकि
ointment	*malaham*	मलहम

HEALTH

patient/sick person	*rogi*	रोगी
sweat (n)	*pasinā*	पसिना
swelling	*sujan*	सुजन
test/examination	*jānc*	जाँच
tetanus	*dhanu rog*	धनुरोग
urine	*pisāb*	पिसाब
vitamin	*bhitāmin*	भिटामिन
vomit (v)	*bāntā garnu*	बान्ता गर्नु

Time, Dates & Festivals

Telling the Time

time	*samay*	समय
What time is it?	*kati bajyo?*	कति बज्यो ?
At what time?	*kati baje tira?*	कति बजेतिर ?
It's two o'clock.	*dui bajyo*	दुई बज्यो
At two o'clock.	*dui baje*	दुई बजे

quarter to two	*paune dui bajyo*	पउने दुई बज्यो
quarter past two	*sawā dui bajyo*	सवा दुई बज्यो
half past two	*sāde dui bajyo*	साँडे दुई बज्यो
(in the) morning	*bihāna*	बिहान
(in the) afternoon	*diunso*	दिउँसो
in the evening	*belukā*	बेलुका
at night	*rāti*	राति

139

TIME, DATES & FESTIVALS

Days of the Week

What day is it today?

	āja ke bār?	आज के बार ?

Monday	*som bār*	सोमबार
Tuesday	*mangal bār*	मंगलबार
Wednesday	*budh bār*	बुधबार
Thursday	*bihi bār*	बिहिबार
Friday	*sukra bār*	शुक्रबार
Saturday	*sani bār*	शनिबार
Sunday	*āita bār*	आईतबार

The Nepali Calendar

In Nepal the Hindu calendar *(bikram samvat)* is used, although in India it is reserved for ritual purposes. It is 57 years ahead of the Gregorian calendar *(isavi san)*, so 1996 AD is 2053 BS. Both have 365 days and 12 months, but the number of days in a Nepali month varies from 29 to 32 and the first Nepali month begins in mid-April.

mid-April to mid-May	*baisākh*	बैशाख
mid-May to mid-June	*jyesth*	ज्येष्ठ
mid-June to mid-July	*āsādh*	आषाढ
mid-July to mid-August	*shrāwan*	श्रावण
mid-Aug to mid-Sept	*bhādra*	भाद्र
mid-Sept to mid-Oct	*āsoj/āshwin*	आशोज / आश्विन
mid-Oct to mid-Nov	*kārtik*	कार्तिक

mid-Nov to mid-Dec	*mangsir*	मंसिर
mid-Dec to mid-Jan	*push*	पौष
mid-Jan to mid-Feb	*māgh*	माघ
mid-Feb to mid-March	*phālgun*	फाल्गुन
mid-March to mid-April	*caitra*	चैत्र

The Bikram calendar uses the word *gate* to indicate the date:

What's the date today?
  āja kati gate?   आज कति गते ?
The first.
  ek gate   एक गते

The Gregorian calendar uses the word *tārikh* to indicate the date:

What's the date today?
  āja kati tārikh?   आज कति तारीख ?
The third.
  tin tārikh   तीन तारीख

Present

today	*āja*	आज
this week	*yo haptā*	यो हप्ता
this morning	*āja bihāna*	आज बिहान
this month	*yo mahinā*	यो महिना
this evening	*āja belukā*	आज बेलुका
this year	*yo barsa*	यो बर्ष
tonight	*āja rāti*	आज राति
now	*ahile*	अहिले

Past

yesterday	hijo	हिजो
yesterday morning	hijo bihāna	हिजो बिहान
day before yesterday/ the other day	asti	अस्ति
last night	hijo rāti	हिजो राति
yesterday evening	hijo belukā	हिजो बेलुका
last week	gayako haptā	गयको हप्ता
last Friday	gayako sukra bār	गयको शुक्रबार

Future

tomorrow	bholi	भोलि
tomorrow night	bholi rāti	भोलि राति
day after tomorrow	parsi	पर्सि
next week	arko haptā	अर्को हप्ता
next month	arko mahinā	अर्को महिना
coming year	āune barsa	आउने बर्ष

Some Useful Words

afternoon	diunso	दिउँसो
century	shatāvdi	शताव्दि
dawn	bihāna saberai	बिहान सबेरै
day	din	दिन
dusk	sandhyākāl	सन्ध्याकाल
early	saberai	सबेरै
evening	belukā	बेलुका
every day	harek din	हरेक दिन
daily	dinhū	दिनहुँ

fortnight (15 days)	*pandhra din*	पन्ध्र दिन
holiday	*bidā*	बिदा
hour	*ghantā*	घण्टा
late	**dhilo**	ढिलो
long ago	*dherai samay bhayo*	धेरै समय भयो
midnight	*madhyarāt*	मध्यरात
minute	*minet*	मिनेट
month	*mahinā*	महिना
morning	*bihāna*	बिहान
never	*kahile hoina*	कहिले होईन
night	*rāti*	राति
noon	*madhyānha*	मध्यानह
public holiday	*sarkāri bidā*	सरकारी बिदा
recently	*hālsālai*	हालसालै
sometimes	*kahile kahĩ*	कहिले कहिं
soon	*cāndai*	चाँडै
week	*haptā*	हप्ता
year	*barsa/sāl*	बर्ष/साल

Some Useful Phrases

When did you come to Nepal?
    *tapāī nepālmā kahileāunu
    bhayako?*   तपाईं नेपालमा कहिले आउनु भयको ?

Two weeks ago.
    dui haptā bhayo   दुई हप्ता भयो

How long will you stay?
    kati basne?   कति बस्ने ?

I'll stay in Nepal for two
years.

ma nepālmā dui barsa baschu   म नेपालमा दुई बर्ष बस्छु

What month is this?

yo mahinā kun ho?   यो महिना कुन हो ?

I'm going to Pokhara for three
weeks.

ma tin haptāko lāgi pokharāmā   म तीन हप्ताको लागि
jānchu   पोखरामा जान्छु

Festivals

There are many gods and religious beings in Nepal, and hundreds of festivals are celebrated every year. The
official religion is Hinduism. It min-
gles harmoniously with Buddhism,
and many religious festivals are celebrated by both Hindus and Buddhists. Festivals are dated according
to the ancient lunar calendar and fall
on days relative to full or new moons.

Most temples are dedicated to one
or other of a multitude of gods, each
known in several forms and by various names. (There are said to be 300
million Hindu deities!) Religion is a
significant part of Nepali culture, and
you will find it easier to gain some
understanding of the culture if you are
familiar with religious and festival
terminology.

Basant Pancami　　　　　बसन्त पंन्चमि
　　January/February – celebration of spring, in honour of
　　Saraswati, the goddess of learning.

Bisket Jātrā　　　　　बिस्कत जात्रा
　　April – feast of the death of the Snake Demons; part of the
　　Nepali New Year.

Buddha Jayanti　　　　बुद्ध जयन्ती
　　April/May – Buddha's birthday.

Caitra Dasain　　　　　चैत्र दशैं
　　March/April – festival dedicated to *Durgā*, exactly six months
　　before the major *Dasain*.

Dasain (Durgā Pujā)　　दशैं (दुर्गा पुजा)
　　September/October – Nepal's biggest annual festival,
　　elebrated in honour of *Durgā's* slaying of the demons. On
　　the eighth day of *Dasain*, sacrifices and offerings to *Durgā*
　　begin. *Navami* is the ninth day of *Dasain* and the main
　　sacrifice day when all Nepalis eat meat. *Bijayā Dashami* is
　　the tenth day of *Dasain*, a family celebration.

Dipāvali　　　　　　　दिपावलि
　　October/November – Festival of Lights; third and most
　　important day of *Tihār*, dedicated to *Laxmi*.

Gunlā　　　　　　　गुंला
　　August/September – special month of Buddhist ceremonies.

Holi　　　　　　　होली
　　February/March – Festival of Colours.

Indra Jātrā　　　　　इन्द्र जात्रा
　　September – festival honouring *Indra*.

Kārtikayā Purnimā　　कार्तिकया पुर्णिमा
　　September/October – full-moon day marking the end of
　　Dasain, celebrated by gambling.

Krishna Jayanti　　　　　　क्रीष्ण जयन्ती
　　August/September – Lord Krishna's birthday; also known as
　　Krishnasthami.

Kumārsāsthi　　　　　　कुमारसास्थी
　　May/June – birthday of *Kārtikayā.*

Losār　　　　　　लोसार
　　February/March – two-week festival for Tibetan New Year.

Māhālaxmi Pujā　　　　　　माहालक्ष्मी पुजा
　　November – harvest festival.

Māni Rimdu Performer

Māni Rimdu　　　　　　मानी रीमदु
　　November – three-day Sherpa festival, held at Thyangpoche
　　monastery in the Solu Khumbu region.

Mha Pujā　　　　　　म्ह पुजा
　　October/November – New Year and day of self-worship for
　　the Newar people.

Nāga Pancami　　　　　　　　　नाग पन्चमी
　　July/August – day of the snake gods who are rain-givers and
　　guardians of water.
Rachā Bandan　　　　　　　　　रक्षाबन्दन
　　August – yellow thread is given out by priests and worn for
　　good luck up until *Tihār* (or for at least a week). Unlike
　　sacred thread, it is available to women and
　　foreigners.
Rāto Machendranāth Jātrā　　　रातो मछेन्द्रनाथ जात्रा
　　April/May – Festival of Red *Machendranāth*; also known as
　　Bhota Jātrā, Festival of the Sacred Vest.
Shivarātri　　　　　　　　　　शिवरात्रि
　　February – *Shiva's* birthday.
Tihār　　　　　　　　　　　　तिहार
　　October/November – second most important Hindu festival
　　in Nepal after *Dasain*, honouring certain animals on succes-
　　sive days. The third day is *Dipāvali*.
Tij　　　　　　　　　　　　　तीज
　　August/September – three-day Festival of Women.

Gods & Prominent Beings

Bhairab　　　　　　　　　　　भैरब
　　Destructive, fearsome form of *Shiva*.
Brāhma　　　　　　　　　　　ब्राम्ह
　　Supreme Being of the Hindu Trinity and Great Creator of
　　all worldly things. His consort is *Saraswati* and his animal is
　　a swan or goose.
Buddha　　　　　　　　　　　बुद्ध
　　The Enlightened One; for Hindus the ninth incarnation of
　　Vishnu.

Durgā दुर्गा

Wrathful, destructive form of *Pārvati*, and killer of demons. *Māhālaxmi* is a form of *Durgā* and one of the eight mother goddesses.

Ganesh गणेश

Elephant-headed god of wisdom, prosperity and success, and remover of obstacles. Elder son of *Shiva* and *Pārvati*, and easily the most popular god in Nepal. Also called *Vinayaka*. His animal is the shrew, a symbol of sagacity.

Garudā गरुदा

Mythical man-bird; mount of *Vishnu*, hater of snakes.

Green Tārā हरियो तारा

Hindu/Buddhist goddess and spiritual consort of the *Dhyani Buddha*.

Hanumān हनुमान

Monkey-faced god/hero of the *Rāmāyānā*, a symbol of friendship. He is trustworthy and alert, and so is often seen as a palace guard.

Indra इन्द्र

Hindu king of the gods and god of rain. His vehicle is an elephant.

Jogini जोगिनी

Mystical goddess and counterpart of *Bhairab*; also known as *Blue Tārā*.

Kāli कालि

Terrifying form of *Pārvati* and goddess of mysteries; the Black Goddess.

Kārtikayā कार्तिकया

Younger son of *Shiva* and *Pārvati*, and younger brother of *Ganesh*. Also known as *Kumār*, he is the god of war and commander of *Shiva's* army. His mount is a peacock.

Krishna　　　　　　　　　　　　क्रीष्ण
　　Eighth incarnation of *Vishnu*, a fun-loving cowherd and
　　hero of the *Mahabharata*. His wife is *Rādhā*.

Laxmi　　　　　　　　　　　　लक्ष्मी
　　Goddess of wealth and prosperity; consort of *Vishnu*.

Machendranāth　　　　　　　　मछेन्द्रनाथ
　　Nepali manifestation of *Avalokiteswara*, protector and god
　　of rains and monsoon.

Māhādevi　　　　　　　　　　माहादेवी
　　Māhādevi is a form of *Pārvati*; *devi* means any female god
　　while *māhā* means 'great'.

Manjushri　　　　　　　　　　मन्जुश्री
　　God of divine wisdom, founder of Nepalese civilisation and
　　creator of the Kathmandu Valley.

Pārvati　　　　　　　　　　　पार्वती
　　Peaceful consort of *Shiva*, representing his female side and,
　　through *Kāli* and *Durgā*, his fearsome side. Her symbol is
　　the yoni, complement to *Shiva's* lingam (see Some Useful
　　Words in this chapter). *Māhādevi* is a form of *Pārvati*.

Pashupati　　　　　　　　　　पशुपति
　　A benevolent form of *Shiva*, lord of beasts and keeper of all
　　living things, and supreme god of Nepal.

Rādhā　　　　　　　　　　　राधा
　　Wife of *Krishna*.

Rāmā　　　　　　　　　　　रामा
　　Seventh incarnation of *Vishnu* and beloved hero of
　　Rāmāyānā. *Rāmā* and his wife *Sita* are Hinduism's favourite
　　romantic couple.

Saraswati　　　　　　　　　　सरस्वती
　　Goddess of learning, intelligence, memory and the creative
　　arts, especially music. Consort of *Brāhma*, she rides a white
　　swan and carries a bina (stringed instrument).

Shakti   शक्ति

Female principle of Supreme Energy. As a god's consort, *Shakti* represents this side of his personality.

Shiva   शिव

Second member of the Hindu Trinity; the destroyer and regenerator who represents time and procreation. The most important god in Nepal, he is often represented by a lingam, his shakti is *Pārvati*, his animal is the bull, *Nandi*, and his common symbols are the trident and drum. His home is Mt Kailash in Tibet. He is supposed to smoke hashish. He is supposed to take thousands of forms, including *Pashupati* and *Bhairab*. *Māhādev*, the great god, is also a manifestation of *Shiva*, and so is *Natarāj*, the god of cosmic dancing.

Sitā   सिता

Wife of *Rāmā* and heroine of the *Rāmāyānā*; symbolises wifely virtue.

Surya   सूर्य

Hindu sun god, also worshipped in Nepal as *Narayan*, who rides a chariot drawn by seven or nine horses. In Buddhism, *Surya* is associated with the moon as a symbol of basic unity.

Taleju   तलेजु

Goddess of the royal family, symbolised by flowers.

Vaishnava

A devotee of *Vishnu*.

Vishnu   विष्णु

Third member of the Hindu trinity; the Preserver. Has appeared on earth in nine incarnations, including the Buddha, with the tenth yet to come. His vehicle is the *Garudā*.

White Tārā सेतो तारा
  Consort of *Avalokiteswara*, protects humans while
  crossing the ocean of existence. Her symbol is a
  full-blown lotus.

Yāmā यामा
  King and judge of the dead; crows are his messengers.

Some Useful Words

āunsi/āmāvasya औंसि/आमावस्य
  the dark moon, a fortnight before the new moon

bāhun बाहुन
  Hindu priest (*Brahmin* in Nepal)

caitya चैत्य
  small, lotus, bud-shaped *stupā*

cānd parba चाँड पब
  festival

cirāg चीराग
  ceremonial oil lamp or torch

deutā देवता
  god/goddess

devadut देवदुट
  mother goddess

dhāmi धामी
  medicine men from the Rai tribe who are also spirit
  mediums and diviners

dharma धर्म
  religious teaching, law and doctrine defining the path to
  universal harmony via individual morals

TIME, DATES & FESTIVALS

ghāt घाट
  riverside platform for cremation, and the name of any
  steps leading down to a river

guru गुरु
  spiritual guide who teaches by inspiring people to follow
  his or her example

jātrā जात्रा
  feast/festival procession

jayanti जयन्ती
  birthday celebration

jhānkri झाँक्री
  hill-dwelling medicine man or faith healer, who performs
  in a trance while beating drums

jivan/jindagi जिवन / जिन्दगी
  life

kāl काल
  death

karma कर्म
  law of cause and effect: actions of all previous lives
  determine the soul's next rebirth

khāt खात
  canopied, ceremonial palanquin for carrying idols

kumāri कुमारी
  young virgin girl, worshipped by Nepalis as a living goddess

lāmā लामा
  spiritual teacher/religious instructor

Lamaism
  Tibetan Tantric Buddhism

lingam लीङ्गम
  phallic symbol of *Shiva* which is commonly used to repre-
  sent him in temples; a symbol of *Shiva's* creative role.

Mahābhārata   महाभारत
   Hindu epic of the battle between two families
mahātmā   महात्मा
   saint
mandalā   मण्डला
   mystic circular design used as a meditation device; a visual
   aid to concentration
mandap   मण्डप
   pavilion
mandir   मन्दिर
   Hindu temple
māni   मानि
   stone with Buddhist prayers carved into it
mantra   मन्त्र
   prayer/invocation/religious incantation/magic spell
melā   मेला
   fair
mokshā   मोक्षा
   spiritual salvation from the cyclic rebirths of reincarnation;
   Hindu equivalent of *nirbhānā*
nirbhānā   निर्भाना
   the eventual aim of all Buddhists: the achievement of a
   state of enlightenment and spiritual peace via the annihila-
   tion of individuality and the end of misery and pain, which
   are caused by desires
pāp   पाप
   sin
prārthanā   प्रार्थना
   prayer
prasād   प्रसाद
   food, sacred after being offered in *pujā*

pujā   पुजा
prayer/worship/religious ceremony

pujāri   पुजारी
priest

purnimā/purna   पुर्णिमा/पुर्ण
bright fortnight preceding full moon

Rāmāyānā   रामायाणा
popular Hindu epic in which the princess, *Sitā,* is abducted
by the evil demon king, *Rawana; Rāmā* and *Hanumān* de-
stroy *Rawana* and rescue *Sitā*

rath   रथ
temple chariot, vehicle of the gods

sādhu   साधु
a Hindu ascetic on a spiritual search, usually a follower of
Shiva carrying a trident

samsāra   समसार
Hindu cycle of transmigration and reincarnation

sangha   संघ
order or community of Buddhist monks

Shaivite
a devotee of *Shiva*

stupā   स्तुपा
Buddhist temple or sanctuary

swastikā   स्वस्तीका
for Hindus, an auspicious sign of law (*swasti* means 'well-
being'); for Buddhists, a symbol of the esoteric doctrine of
the Buddha

tantra   तन्त्र
esoteric, psycho-sexual, mystic philosophy which leads to
enlightenment; a major influence on Nepalese Hinduism
and Buddhism.

Tārā तारा
　the Hindu/Buddhist female principle which has many forms

tikā तीका
　auspicious mark of red vermilion sindur paste, placed on
　the forehead during *pujā* or festivals

vahānā वहाना
　animal that acts as a vehicle of a Hindu god

vajra वज्र
　thunderbolt or diamond; symbol of Tantric Buddhism. It
　destroys ignorance and symbolises purity and indestruct-
　ibility and it represents *nirbhānā*; male complement of
　the female principle, *ghanta*

vajrācārya वज्राचार्य
　Buddhist Newar priest

yānā याना
　way, path or vehicle to Buddhist enlightenment

yogi योगि
　holy man

yoni योनी
　plate-like disc with drain, representing
　the female sexual organ; symbol of
　Pārvati which is often found in combi-
　nation with a lingam and acts as a
　reservoir for offerings.

Numbers & Amounts

Cardinal Numbers

0	*sunya*	शून्य		15	*pandhra*	पन्ध्र
1	*ek*	एक		16	*sorha*	सोह्
2	*dui*	दुई		17	*satra*	सत्र
3	*tin*	तीन		18	*athāra*	अठार
4	*cār*	चार		19	*unnāis*	उन्नाईस
5	*pānc*	पाँच		20	*bis*	बीस
6	*cha*	छ		30	*tis*	तीस
7	*sāt*	सात		40	*cālis*	चालीस
8	*āth*	आठ		50	*pacās*	पचास
9	*nau*	नौ		60	*sātthi*	साठ्ठी
10	*das*	दश		70	*sattari*	सत्तरी
11	*eghāra*	एघार		80	*asshi*	अस्सी
12	*bārha*	बाह्		90	*nabbe*	नब्बे
13	*terha*	तेह्		100	*ek say*	एक शय
14	*caudha*	चौध				

156

1000	*ek hajār*	एक हजार
10 000	*das hajār*	दश हजार
100 000	*ek lākh*	एक लाख
one million	*das lākh*	दश लाख
ten million	*ek karoḍ*	एक करोड

Ordinal Numbers

These are formed by adding *-aū* to the number. The first four are irregular:

1st	*pahilā*	पहिला
2nd	*dosrā*	दोस्रा
3rd	*tesrā*	तेस्रा
4th	*cauntho*	चौंठो
5th	*pāncaū*	पाँचौं
10th	*dasaū*	दशौं
20th	*bisaū*	बीसौं

Counters

When counting people or things in Nepali, special words must be used between the number and the noun. These words are called counters. The counter for things is *watā*; for people *janā*, but informally *watā* is also used for people. Think of these counters as part of the number; like saying 'two *sheets* of paper' or 'two *slices* of bread'. The thing or person being counted always stays in the singular. The counters for numbers 1-3 are irregular.

one	*ek*	एक	one (thing)	*eutā*	एउटा
two	*dui*	दुई	two (things)	*duitā*	दुईटा
three	*tin*	तीन	three (things)	*tintā*	तीनटा

four	*cār*	चार	four (things)	*cār watā*	चार वटा
five	*pānc*	पाँच	five (things)	*pānc watā*	पाँच वटा
ten	*das*	दश	ten (things)	*das watā*	दश वटा
twenty	*bis*	बीस	twenty (things)	*bis watā*	बीस वटा

How many (things)?
   kati watā?   कति वटा ?
How many (people)?
   kati janā?   कति जना ?

apple	*syāu*	स्याउ
two apples	*duitā syāu*	दुईटा स्याउ
tiger	*bāgh*	बाघ
five tigers	*pānc watā bāgh*	पाँच वटा बाघ
person	*mānche*	मान्छे
one person	*ek janā mānche*	एक जना मान्छे
sister	*bahini*	बहिनी
three sisters	*tin janā bahini*	तीन जना बहिनी

To make a multiple, add *-palta* to the number:

| twice | *dui palta* | दुई पल्ट |
| three times | *tin palta* | तीन पल्ट |

Fractions

¼	*pāu*	पाउ
⅓	*tihāi*	तीहाई
½	*ādhā*	आधा
2½	*adhāi*	अधाई

Vocabulary

A

able (to be)	*saknu*	स
above	*māthi*	माथि
accept (v)	*mānnu*	मान्नु
I accept	*ma mānchu*	म मान्छु
Do you accept?	*tapāī mānnu huncha?*	तपाईं मान्नुहुन्छ ?
accident	*durghatanā*	दुर्घटना
address	*thegānā*	ठेगाना
administration	*prasāsan*	प्रशासन
advice	*sallāha*	सल्लाह
advise	*sallāha dinu*	सल्लाह दिनु
afraid (to be)	*darnu*	डर्नु
after	*pachi*	पछि
again	*pheri*	फेरी
age	*umer*	उमेर
agree	*manjur garnu*	मन्जुर गर्नु
I agree.	*ma manjur garchu*	म मन्जुर गर्छु
Do you agree?	*tapāī manjur garnu huncha?*	तपाईं मन्जुर गर्नुहुन्छ ?
agriculture	*khetipāti*	खेतीपाती
aid	*sahayog*	सहयोग
air	*hāwā*	हावा
air-conditioned	*bātānukulit*	बातानुकुलीत

159

airmail	*hawāi dāk*	हवाइडाक
all	*sabai*	सबै
almost	*jhandai*	झन्डै
alone	*eklai*	हवाइडाक
along	*bhari*	भरि
also/too	*pani*	पनि
alternative	*upāya*	उपाय
always	*sadhaĩ*	सधैं
ambassador	*rājdut*	राजदूत
among	*madhye*	मध्ये
ancient	*prācin*	प्राचीन
and	*ra*	र
and then/and so	*ani*	अनि
anger	*ris*	रिस
angry (to be)	*risāunu*	रिसाउनु
animal	*janāwar*	जनावर
annoyance	*dikka*	दिक्क
answer (v)	*jawāph dinu*	जवाफ दिनु
anyone	*kohi*	कोही
anything	*kehi*	केही
anywhere	*jahā̃*	जहाँ
apartment	*derā*	डेरा
appointment	*bhet garne samaya*	भेट गर्ने समय
(meeting time)		
approximately	*lagbhag*	लगभग
argue	*bahas garnu*	बहस गर्नु
argument	*bahas*	बहस
arrive	*pugnu*	पुग्नु
art	*kalā*	कला

ask	*sodhnu*	सोध्नु
ask for	*māgnu*	माग्नु
at	*mā*	मा
autorickshaw	*tyāmpu*	टयाम्पु
autumn	*sharad ritu*	शरद ऋतु
(is) available	*pāincha*	पाइन्छ

B

baby	*baccā*	बच्चा
baby's bottle	*dudh khuwāune sisi*	दूध खुवाउने सिसी
bad	*kharāb*	खराब
bag/pack	*jholā*	झोला
balcony	*bārdali*	बार्दली
ball	*bhakundo*	भकुन्डो
bandage	*patti*	पट्टी
barber	*hajām*	हजाम
bargain (v)	*moltol garnu*	मोलतोल गर्नु
basket	*tokari*	टोकरी
bathe	*nuhāunu*	नुहाउनु
battery	*masalā*	मसला
be (v)	*hunu*	हुनु
beach/seaside	*samudrako kināra*	समुद्रको किनार
beautiful	*sundar*	सुन्दर
because	*kinabhane*	किनभने
bed	*khāt*	खाट
bedbug	*udus*	उड्स
before	*aghi*	अघि
beggar	*māgne mānche*	माग्ने मान्छे

begin	*suru garnu*	सुरु गर्नु
behind/back	*pachādi*	पछाडि
belief	*bishwās*	बिश्वास
believe	*bishwās garnu*	बिश्वास गर्नु
below	*tala*	तल
beside	*cheumā*	छेउमा
best	*sab-bhandā rāmro*	सबभन्दा राम्रो
between	*bicmā*	बीचमा
big	*thulo*	ठूलो
bill	*bil*	बिल
birthday (official)	*jayanti*	जयन्ती
birthday (personal)	*janma din*	जन्मदिन
blanket	*kambal*	कम्बल
blessing	*āsik*	आसिक
blind	*andho*	अन्धो
blizzard	*hiūko āndhi*	हिउँको आँधी
boat	*dungā*	डुङ्गा
body	*sharir/jiu*	शरीर / जीउ
book	*kitāb*	किताब
border	*simānā*	सिमाना
bored (to be)	*wākka hunu*	वाक्क हुनु
borrow	*sāpat linu*	सापट लिनु
boss	*mālik*	मालिक
both	*dubai*	दुबै
bottle	*sisi*	सिसी
box	*bākas*	बाकस
boy	*ketā*	केटा
boyfriend	*premi*	प्रेमि

break (v)	*phutāunu*	फुटाउनु
breathe	*sās phernu*	सास फेर्नु
bribe (n)	*ghus*	घुस
bridge	*pul*	पुल
bring	*lyāunu*	ल्याउनु
broken	*phutyo*	फुट्यो
brother (elder)	*dāi*	दाइ
(younger)	*bhāi*	भाइ
bucket	*bāltin*	बाल्टिन
Buddhism	*buddha dharma*	बौद्ध धर्म
building	*bhawan*	भवन
burn (v)	*polnu*	पोल्नु
bus	*bas*	बस
bush/shrub	*bota*	बोट
busy	*besta*	बेस्त
but	*tara*	तर
buy	*kinnu*	किन्नु
by	*-le*	-ले

C

calendar	*sambat*	सम्बत्
call	*bolāunu*	बोलाउनु
camp (v)	*shivir garnu*	शिविर गर्नु
cancel	*radda garnu*	रद्द गर्नु
can (able to)	*saknu*	सक्नु
can (n)	*tin*	टिन
can opener	*tin kholne*	टिन खोल्ने
candle	*mainbatti*	मैनबत्ती

capital city	rājdhāni	राजधानी
capitalism	punjivād	पूँजीवाद
car	moṭar	मोटर
(playing) cards	tās	तास
careful (to be)	hos garnu	होस गर्नु
carry	boknu	बोक्नु
cave	guphā	गुफा
cemetery	cihān	चिहान
century	shatāvdi	शताव्दि
certain	pakkā/niscaya	पक्का / निश्चय
chair	mec	मेच
chance	dāu	दाउ
change (money)	sāṭnu	साट्नु
cheap	sasto	सस्तो
check (v)	jāncnu	जाँच्नु
chemist	ausadhi pasal	औषधी पसल
children	keṭākeṭi	केटाकेटी
(one's own)	chorāchori	छोराछोरी
choose	chānnu	छान्नु
cigarette	curoṭ	चुरोट
citizen	nāgarik	नागरिक
city	shahar	शहर
clean (v)	saphā garnu	सफा गर्नु
climb (v)	caḍhnu	चढ्नु
clinic	cikitsālaya	चिकित्सालय
clock	bhitte ghaḍi	भित्ते घडी
close (v)	banda garnu	बन्द गर्नु
clothing	lugā	लुगा
cloud	bādal	बादल

cloudy	*badali*	बदली
coin	*mudrā*	मुद्रा
cold (weather)	*jādo*	जाडो
cold (touch)	*ciso*	चिसो
cold (virus)	*rughā*	रुघा
collect (v)	*lina āunu*	लिन आउनु
colour	*rang*	रङ्ग
come	*āunu*	आउनु
comfortable	*ārām*	आराम
communism	*sāmyavād*	साम्यवाद
condom	*dhāl*	ढाल
confirm	*pakkā garnu*	पक्का गर्नु
contaminated	*jhuto*	झूटो
conversation	*kurā kāni*	कुराकानी
cook (n)	*bhānche*	भान्छे
cook (v)	*pakāunu*	पकाउनु
cool	*shital*	शीतल
cooperative (n)	*sājhā*	साझा
corner	*kunā*	कुना
corruption	*bhrastācār*	भ्रष्टाचार
count (v)	*gannu*	गन्नु
country	*desh*	देश
crazy	*baulāhā*	बौलाहा
credit card	*kreditkard*	क्रेडीटकर्ड
cremation	*dāha sanskār*	दाह संस्कार
crop	*bāli*	बाली
crowd	*hul*	हूल
cultivate	*khanjot garnu*	खनजोत गर्नु
cultural show	*sānskritik*	सांस्क्रितिक

	pradarshan	प्रदर्शन
culture	*sanskriti*	संस्कृति
cup	*kap*	कप
cupboard	*darāj*	दराज
curtain	*pardā*	पर्दा
customs	*bhansār*	भन्सार
cut (n)	*ghāu*	घाउ

D

daily	*dinhū*	दिनहुँ
damp	*osilo*	ओसिलो
dance (v)	*nācnu*	नाच्नु
dancer	*nācne mānche*	नाच्ने मान्छे
danger	*khatarā*	खतरा
dark	*andhyāro*	अँध्यारो
dark moon	*aunsi*	औंसी
date	*gate/tārikh*	गते / तारिख
dawn	*bihān*	बिहान्
day	*din/bār*	दिन / बार
dead	*mareko*	मरेको
decide	*nirnaya garnu*	निर्णय गर्नु
delayed	**dhilo**	ढिलो
democracy	*prajātantra*	प्रजातन्त्र
demonstration/ protest march	*julus*	जुलूस
deny	*namānnu*	नमान्नु
depart	*prasthān garnu*	प्रस्थान गर्नु
departure	*prasthān*	प्रस्थान

destroy	*nās garnu*	नाश गर्नु
detail (v)	*varnan garnu*	वर्णन गर्नु
development	*bikās*	बिकास
dictatorship	*tānāshāhi*	तानाशाही
dictionary	*shabda kosh*	शब्दकोश
die	*marnu*	मर्नु
different	*pharak*	फरक
difficult	*gāhro*	गाह्रो
dinner	*bhāt*	भात
direction	*dishā*	दिशा
dirty	*phohor*	फोहोर
disadvantage	*bephāidā*	बेफाइदा
discount (n)	*chut*	छुट
discover	*pattā lāunu*	पत्ता लाउनु
discrimination	*pachapāt*	पक्षपात
do (v)	*garnu*	गर्नु
doctor	**dā**k*tar*	डक्टर
door/gate	**dh**okā	ढोका
down	*tala*	तल
downhill	*orālo*	ओरालो
downward	*talatira*	तलतिर
dozen	*darjan*	दर्जन
dream (n)	*sapanā*	सपना
drink (v)	*piunu*	पिउनु
drinking water	*khāne pāni*	खाने पानी
drive (v)	*hānknu*	हाँक्न
drug	*okhati*	ओखती
drunk	*raksi lāgyo*	रक्सी लाग्यो

| dusk | *sandhyākāl* | सन्ध्याकाल |
| dust | *dhulo* | धूलो |

E

each/every	*harek*	हरेक
early	*saberai/cāndai*	सबेरै / चाँडै
earn	*kamāunu*	कमाउनु
earth	*prithivi*	प्रिथिवी
earthquake	*bhuincālo*	भुईंचालो
east	*purba*	पूर्ब
easy	*sajilo*	सजिलो
eat	*khānu*	खानु
economical	*kamkharcilo*	कमखर्चिलो
economy	*artha byabasthā*	अर्थ व्यवस्था
education	*shichā*	शिक्षा
election	*cunāb*	चुनाब
electricity	*bijuli*	बिजुली
else	*aru*	अरु
embarrassed/ ashamed	*lajjit*	लज्जीत
embassy	*rājdutāvās*	राजदूतावास
employer	*mālik/ mālikni*	मालिक (m)/ मालिकनी (f)
empty	*khāli*	खाली
end (n)	*anta*	अन्त
energy/power	*shakti*	शक्ति
English	*angreji*	अंग्रेजी
enjoy	*ānanda linu*	आनन्द लिनु

enough	*prashasta*	प्रशस्त
enter	*pasnu*	पस्नु
Do not enter.	*prabesh nagarnu*	प्रबेश नगर्नु
envelope	*khām*	खाम
equal	*barābar*	बराबर
even (number)	*jor*	जोर
event	*ghatanā*	घटना
exactly	*thik*	ठीक
exile	*desh nikālā*	देश निकाला
expect	*apechā garnu*	अपेक्षा गर्नु
expensive	*mahango*	महँगो
experience (n)	*anubhav*	अनुभव
experience (v)	*anubhav garnu*	अनुभव गर्नु
export (n)	*niryāt*	निर्यात
export (v)	*niryāt garnu*	निर्यात गर्नु

F

factory	*kārakhānā*	कारखाना
fair/market	*mela*	मेल
faith	*bishwās*	बिश्वाश
fall (v)	*khasnu*	खस्नु
ffamily	*paribār*	परिबार
fan (n)	*pankhā*	पंखा
far	*tādhā*	टाढा
farm	*khetbāri*	खेतबारी
farmer	*kisān*	किसान
fast	*chito/cāndai*	छिटो / चाँडै
fast (n)	*vrata*	व्रत

fat	*moto*	मोटो
fear (n)	**dar**	डर
fear (v)	*darnu*	डर्नु
fee	*shulka*	शुल्क
feel (like doing)	*man lāgnu*	मनलाग्नु
female	*pothi*	पोथि
festival	*cādbād/jātrā*	चाडबाड/जात्रा
few	*thorai*	थोरै
field	*khet*	खेत
fight (v)	*ladnu*	लड्नु
film (movie)	*calacitra*	चलचित्र
film (colour)	*rangin ril*	रंङ्गीन रील
(B&W)	*kālo seto ril*	कालोसेतो रील
firewood	*dāurā*	दाउरा
first	*pahilā*	पहिला
flag	*jhandā*	झन्डा
flashlight/torch	*tarclāit*	टर्चलाईट
flight	*udān*	उडान
food	*khānā*	खाना
food poisoning	*khānā kharāb*	खाना खराब
(on) foot	*hīdera*	हिंडेर
for	*-ko lāgi*	को लागि
foreign/foreigner	*bideshi*	बिदेशी
forest	*ban*	बन
forever	*sadhaĩ*	सधैँ
forget	*birsanu*	बिर्सनु
I forgot.	*maile birsyo*	मैले बिर्स्यो
forgive	*māph garnu*	माफ गर्नु
fortnight	*pandhra din*	पन्ध्र दिन

free (gratis)	*sittain*	सित्तैं
free (not bound)	*swatantra*	स्वतन्त्र
freedom	*swatantratā*	स्वतन्त्रता
friend	*sāthi*	साथी
friendly	*milansār*	मिलनसार
frighten	*darāunu*	डराउनु
from (place)	*bāta*	बाट
(time)	*dekhi*	देखि
(in) front (of)	*agādi*	अगाडि
frost	*tusāro*	तुसारो
frostbite	*tusārole khāyako*	तुसारोले खायको
fun	*majjā*	मज्जा
future	*bhabisya*	भबिष्य

G

game	*khel*	खेल
garbage	*mailā*	मैला
garden	*bagaincā*	बगैंचा
gas	*gyās*	ग्याँस
gas cylinder	*gyās silindar*	ग्याँस सिलिन्डर
gate/door	*dhokā*	ढोका
gem	*juhārāt*	जुहारात
girl	*keti*	केटी
girlfriend	*premikā*	प्रेमिका
give	*dinu*	दिनु
Please give me ...	*malāi ... dinuhos*	मलाई ... दिनुहोस
glass	*gilās*	गिलास
go	*jānu*	जानु
I'm going to ...	*ma ... mā jāndaichu*	म ... मा जान्दैछु

go (on foot)	*hĩdera jānu*	हिंडेर जानु
god/goddess	*deutā*	देवता
gold	*sun*	सुन
good	*rāmro/asal*	राम्रो/असल
Goodbye.	*namaste/*	नमस्ते
	namaskār	नमस्कार
goods	*sāmān*	सामान
government	*sarkār*	सरकार
grateful	*kritagya*	क्रितज्ञ
greedy	*lobhi*	लोभी
grow (in size)	*badhnu*	बढ्नु
grow (something)	*ubjāunu*	उब्जाउनु
guess (n)	*andāj*	अन्दाज
guess (v)	*andāj garnu*	अन्दाज गर्नु
guesthouse	*pāhunā ghar*	पाहुनाघर
guide (trekking)	*bāto dekhāune*	बाटो देखाउने
	mānche	मान्छे
guidebook	*nirdeshanko kitāb*	निर्देशनको किताब
guilty	*doshi*	दोषी

H

habit	*bāni*	बानी
half	*ādhā*	आधा
handkerchief	*rumāl*	रुमाल
handmade	*hātle baneko*	हातले बनेको
happy	*khusi*	खुसी
hard (difficult)	*gāhro*	गाह्रो
hard (not soft)	*kadā*	कडा
hashish	*cares*	चरेस

hat	*topi*	टोपी
headstrap	*nāmlo*	नाम्लो
health post (clinic)	*cikitsālaya*	चिकित्सालय
hear/listen to	*sunnu*	सुन्नु
heart	*mutu*	मुटु
heat	*tāp*	ताप
heater (electric)	*hitar*	हिटर
heaven	*swarga*	सर्वग
heavy	*gahraũ*	गह्रौं
hell	*narak*	नरक
Hello.	*namaste/namaskār*	नमस्त / नमस्कार
help (v)	*maddat garnu*	मद्दत गर्नु
Help!	*guhār!*	गुहार !
hemp	*bhāng*	भाङ्ग
here	*yahā̃*	यहाँ
high	*ucco*	उच्चो
hill	*pahād*	पहाड
hillperson	*pahādi*	पहाडी
hire	*bhādāmā linu*	भाँडामा लिनु
I want to hire ...	*ma ... bhādāmā linchu*	म ... भाँडामा लिन्छु
hole	*pwāl*	प्वाल
holiday	*bidā*	बिदा
holy	*pabitra*	पबित्र
homosexuality	*samalinga sambhogatā*	संमलिङ्ग संभोगता
honest	*imāndār*	ईमान्दार
hookah	*hukkhā*	हुक्खा
hospital	*aspatāl*	अस्पताल

hospitality	*byabahār*	ब्यबहार
hot (weather)	*garmi*	गर्मि
hot (touch)	*tāto*	तातो
hotel	*hotel*	होटेल
hour	*ghantā*	घण्टा
house/home	*ghar*	घर
how	*kasari*	कसरी
How much/many?	*kati*	कति
human (n)	*mānis*	मानिस
humid	*bāspiya*	बाष्पीय
hunger	*bhok*	भोक
I'm hungry.	*malāi bhok lāgyo*	मलाई भोक लाग्यो
Are you hungry?	*tapāī lāi bhok lāgyo?*	तपाईलाई भोक लाग्यो ?
hurry (v)	*chito garnu*	छिटो गर्नु
(in a) hurry	*hatār*	हतार
hurt (someone)	*cot lagāunu*	चोट लगाउनु
hurt (be hurting)	*dukhnu*	दुख्नु
hut	*jhupro*	झुप्रो

I

I	*ma*	म
ice	*baraph*	बरफ
ice peak	*himāl*	हिमाल
idea	*bicār*	बिचार
identity	*paricaya*	परिचय
idol/statue	*murti*	मूर्ति
if	*yadi*	यॊदि
ill	*birāmi*	बिरामि

illegal	*abaidh*	अबैध
illness	*rog*	रोग
imagination	*kalpanā*	कल्पना
imitation	*nakkal*	नक्कल
immediately	*turuntai*	तुरुन्तै
import (n)	*āyāt*	आयात
import (v)	*āyāt garnu*	आयात गर्नु
impossible	*asambhab*	असम्भव
imprisonment	*kārābās*	कारावास
in	*-mā*	–मा
incense burner	*dhup dāni*	धुप दानि
including	*samet*	समेत
inconvenient	*asubidhā*	असुबिधा
industry	*udyog*	उद्योग
informal	*anaupacārik*	अनौपचारिक
information	*sucanā/khabar*	सुचना / खबर
in front of	*agādi*	अगाडि
injury	*cot patak*	चोटपटक
inn	*bhatti*	भत्ति
intellect	*buddhi*	बुद्धि
interest/hobby	*cākh*	चाख
interesting	*cākh lāgdo*	चाख लाग्दो
invite	*nimtā garnu*	निम्ता गर्नु
it	*tyo/yo*	त्यो / यो

J

jail	*jhyāl khānā*	झयालखाना
jewellery	*gahanā*	गहना
job	*kām*	काम

joint	*jorni*	जोर्नी
joke	*khyāl/thattā*	ख्याल / ठट्टा
I'm joking.	*maile khyāl gareko*	मैले ख्याल गरेको
journey	*yātrā*	यात्रा
jump (v)	*uphranu*	उफ्रनु
jungle	*ban*	बन

K

kerosene	*mati tel*	मटीतेल
kill (v)	*mārnu*	मार्नु
kindness	*dayā*	दया
king	*rājā*	राजा
kiss (n)	*mwāi*	म्वाई
knife	*cakku/khukuri*	चक्कु / खुकुरी
know (person)	*cinnu*	चीन्नु
(thing)	*thāhā pāunu*	थाहापाउनु
knowledge	*gyān*	ज्ञान

L

lake	*tāl*	ताल
lamp/light	*batti*	बत्ती
lamp/torch (ceremonial)	*cirāg*	चीराग
lamp (sacred butter)	*dip*	दिप
landslide	*pahiro*	पहिरो
language	*bhāsā*	भाषा
last	*antim/gayako*	अन्तीम / गयको
late	**d**hilo/aberai	ढिलो / अबेरै

laugh (v)	*hāsnu*	हाँस्नु
laundry	*lugā dhune thāũ*	लुगाधुने ठाउँ
lazy	*alchi*	अल्छी
learn (v)	*siknu*	सिक्न
leather	*chālā*	छाला
leave	*chodnu*	छोड्नु
left (direction)	*bāyā̃*	बायाँ
legal	*kānuni*	कानूनी
letter	*citthi*	चिठ्ठी
level	*samma*	सम्म
library	*pustakālaya*	पुस्तकालय
lie (v)	*dhā̃tnu*	ढाँट्नु
life	*jindagi*	जिन्दगी
light (colour)	*ujyālo*	उज्यालो
light (weight)	*halukā*	हलुका
lightning	*bijuli camkāi*	बिजुली चम्काई
like (v)	*man parnu*	मनपर्नु
I like/don't like ...	*malāi ... man parcha/pardaina*	मलाई ... मनपर्छ / मनपर्दैन
listen	*sunnu*	सुन्नु
(a) little	*ali ali/alikati*	अलि अलि / अलिकति
live (v)	*basnu*	बस्नु
load	*bhāri*	भारी
lock (v)	*tālcā lāunu*	ताल्चा लाउनु
lodge	*laj*	लज
long	*lāmo*	लामो
look (v)	*hernu*	हेर्नु
look for	*khojnu*	खोज्नु
loose	*khukulo*	खुकुलो

lose	*harāunu*	हराउनु
lost	*harāuna*	हराउन
I'm lost.	*ma harāyē*	म हरायें
loud	**thulo**	ठूलो
love	**māyā**	माया
(romantic)	*prem*	प्रेम
I love you.	*ma tapāīlāi māyā/*	म तपाईंलाई माया/
	prem garchu	प्रेम गर्छु
low	**hoco**	होचो
lucky	**bhāgyamāni**	भाग्यमानी
luggage	**sāmān**	सामान
lunch	**camenā**	चमेना

M

machine	**kal**	कल
magazine	**patra patrikā**	पत्रपत्रिका
majority	**dheraijaso**	धेरैजसो
make (v)	**banāunu**	बनाउनु
male	**bhāle**	भाले
many/much	**dherai**	धेरै
map	**naksā**	नक्सा
marijuana	**gānjā**	गाँजा
market	**bajār**	बजार
marriage	**bibāha**	बिबाह
mask	**makundo**	मकुण्डो
massage (n)	**mālis**	मालीस
mat	**gundari**	गुन्द्री
matches	**salāi**	सलाई
mattress	**dasanā**	डसना

maybe	*shāyad*	शायद
meal	*khānā*	खाना
measure (v)	*nāpnu*	नाप्नु
meat	*māsu*	मासु
meet	*bhetnu*	भेट्नु
I'll meet you.	*ma tapāīlāi bhetchu*	म तपाईंलाई भेट्छु
melt	*pagālnu*	पगाल्नु
menu/index	*suci*	सूची
message	*khabar*	खबर
midnight	*madhyarāt*	मध्यरात
minute	*minet*	मिनेट
mirror	*ainā*	ऐना
mistake	*galti*	गल्ती
mix (something)	*misāunu*	मिसाउन्नु
modern	*ādhunik*	आधुनिक
moment	*ek chin*	एकछिन
monastery	*gumbā*	गुम्बा
money	*paisā*	पैसा
monsoon	*barsāyukta hāwā*	बर्षायुक्त हावा
month	*mahinā*	महिना
monument	*smārak*	स्मारक
moon	*candramā*	चन्द्रमा
full moon	*purnimā*	पूर्णिमा
dark moon	*aunsi/amavasya*	औंसि / अमवस्य
morning	*bihāna*	बिहान
mosque	*masjid*	मस्जिद
mountain	*himāl*	हिमाल
mountaineer	*parbatārohi*	पर्वतारोही

mouth	*mukh*	मुख
move (something)	*calāunu*	चलाउनु
mud	*hilo*	हिलो
museum	*samgrahālaya*	संग्रहालय
music	*sangit*	संङ्गीत
my/mine	*mero*	मेरो

N

name	*nām*	नाम
napkin	*rumāl*	रुमाल
narcotic	*lāgu ausadhi*	लागु औषधी
narrow	*sānghuro*	साँघुरो
nature	*prakriti*	प्रक्रिति
near	*najik*	नजिक
nearest	*najikai*	नजिकै
necessary	*ābashyak*	आवश्यक
needed	*cāhinu*	चाहिनु
needle/syringe	*siyo*	सियो
neither ... nor ...	*na ... na ...*	न ... न ...
net	*jāl*	जाल
never	*kahile hoina*	कहिले होईन
new	*nayā̃*	नयाँ
news	*samācār*	समाचार
newspaper	*akhabār*	अखबार
next	*arko/āune*	अर्को / आउने
night	*rāt*	रात
no	*hoina/chaina*	होईन / छैन
noise	*āwāj*	आवाज
noisy	*hallā*	हल्ला

noon	*madhyānha*	मध्यान्ह
no one	*kohi (pani)*	कोहि (पनि)
north	*uttar*	उत्तर
notebook	*kāpi*	कापि
nothing	*kehi (pani)*	केहि (पनि)
now	*ahile*	अहिले
nowadays	*acel*	अचेल
number	*nambar*	नम्बर

O

obvious	*spasta*	स्पष्ट
ocean	*mahāsāgar*	महासागर
occupation	*peshā*	पेशा
odd (number)	*bijor*	बिजोर
of	*-ko*	–को
offend	*apamān garnu*	अपमान गर्नु
offer (v)	*dinu*	दिनु
office	*kāryālaya*	कार्यालय
often	*aksar*	अक्सर
Oh!	*aoho/e!*	ओहो/ऐ !
oil	*tel*	तेल
OK.	*thikcha/huncha/hās*	ठीकछ/हुन्छ/हास
old (person)	*budha/budhi*	बुढा/बुढी
old (thing)	*purāno*	पुरानो
on	*-mā*	–मा
once	*ek coti*	एकचोटी
only	*mātrai*	मात्रै
open (v)	*kholnu*	खोल्नु
opinion	*rāya*	राय

opportunity	*maukā*	मौका
opposite (antithesis)	*biparit*	विपरीत
opposite (other side)	*ulto*	उल्टो
or	*ki*	कि
ordinary	*sādhāran*	साधारण
organisation	*sangha*	संघ
organise	*bandobasta milāunu*	वन्दोवस्त मिलाउनु
ornament	*gahanā*	गहना
other	*arko/aru*	अर्को/अरु
otherwise	*natra*	नत्र
out/outside	*bāhira*	बाहिर
over	*māthi*	माथि
overnight	*rāt bhari*	रातभरि
overseas	*bideshmā*	बिदेशमा
over there	*u tyahā̃*	उ त्यहाँ
owe	*rina lāgnu*	ऋण लाग्नु
I owe you.	*ma tapāĩlāi rina lāgyo*	म तपाईलाई ऋण लाग्यो
You owe me.	*tapāĩ malāi rina lāgyo*	तपाई मलाई ऋण लाग्यो
own (adj)	*āphno*	आफ्नो
owner	*sāhu(-ji/-ni)*	साहु(-जी/-नी)
oxygen	*prānbāyu*	प्राणवायु

P

| packet | *poko/battā* | पोको/बट्टा |
| pagoda | *gajur* | गजुर |

pain	dukhāi	दुखाई
pair	jor	जोर
painting	calacitra/thāngkā	चलचित्र / थाङ्का
palace	darbār	दरबार
paper	kāgaj	कागज
Pardon?	hajur?	हजुर ?
parliament	samsad	संसद
participate	bhāg linu	भाग लिनु
particular	bishes	बिशेष
party (feast)	bhoj	भोज
party (political)	dala	दल
pass	bhanjyāng	भंज्याङ्ग
passenger	yātri	यात्री
passport	rāhadāni	राहदानी
past (time)	bhutkāl	भूतकाल
pay (v)	tirnu	तिर्नु
peace	shānti	शान्ति
peak	cucuro	चुचुरो
pedestrian	paidal yātri	पैदलयात्री
pen	kalam	कलम
pencil	sisākalam	सिसाकलम
people	māncheharu/janatā	मान्छेहरु / जनता
per cent	pratishat	प्रतिशत
perfect	atyutam	अत्युतम
permanent	sthāyi	स्थायी
permission	anumati	अनुमति
permit (v)	anumati dinu	अनुमति दिनु
personal	byaktigat	व्यक्तिगत

pet (n)	*pāltu janāwar*	पाल्तु जनावर
pharmacy	*ausadhi pasal*	औषाधी पसल
phone (v)	*phon garnu*	फोन गर्नु
photo	*tasbir*	तस्बीर
May I take your photo?	*tapāīko tasbir khicnu huncha?*	तपाईंको तस्बीर खिच्नुहुन्छ ?
pick up (v)	*lina āunu*	लिन आउनु
piece	*tukrā*	टुक्रा
pipe	*curot pāip*	चुरोट पाईप
place	*thāū*	ठाउँ
plains	*madesh/tarāi*	मदेश / तराई
plainsdweller	*madeshi*	मदेशी
plant (n)	*biruwā*	बिरुवा
platform (for cremation)	*ghat*	घाट
play (v)	*khelnu*	खेल्नु
player	*khelādi*	खेलाडि
point (out)	*dekhāunu*	देखाउनु
police	*prahari*	प्रहरी
politics	*rājniti*	राजनीति
poor	*garib*	गरीब
positive (certain)	*niscaya*	निश्चय
positive (good)	*sakārātmak*	सकारात्मक
post office	*hulāk addā*	हुलाक अड्डा
pottery	*mātoko sāmān*	माटोको सामान
poverty	*daridratā*	दरिद्रता
power	*shakti*	शक्ति
prayer	*pujā/mantra/ prārthanā*	पुजा / मन्त्र / प्रार्थना

prayer wheel	*māne*	माने
prefer	*bes lāgnu*	बेस लाग्नु
pregnant	*garbhavati*	गर्भवती
prepare	*tayār garnu*	तयार गर्नु
present (time)	*bartamān samaya*	बर्तमान समय
president	*rāstrapati*	राष्ट्रपति
pressure	*dabād*	दबाद
prevent	*roknu*	रोक्नु
price	*mol*	मोल
pride	*garba*	गर्व
priest	*pujāri*	पूजारी
prime minister	*pradhān mantri*	प्रधानमन्त्री
prison	*jhyāl khānā*	झयालखाना
prisoner	*kaid*	कैद
private	*niji*	निजी
problem	*samasyā*	समस्या
process (n)	*kāmko bidhi*	कामको बिधि
process (v)	*prakriyā calāunu*	प्रक्रिया चलाउनु
procession	*julus*	जुलुस
(wedding)	*janti*	जन्ती
produce (n)	*utpādan*	उत्पादन
produce (v)	*utpādan garnu*	उत्पादन गर्नु
profit (n)	*nāphā*	नाफा
promise (n)	*bacan*	बचन
promise (v)	*bacan dinu*	बचन दिनु
proprietor	*sāhuji/sāhuni*	साहुजी (m) / साहुनी (f)
prostitute	*beshyā*	बेश्या
protect	*bacāunu*	बचाउनु

protest (n)	*birodh*	बिरोध
public (adj)	*sārbajanik*	सार्वजनिक
pull	*tānnu*	तान्नु
push (v)	*ghacetnu*	घचेट्नु
put	*rākhnu*	राख्नु

Q

quality	*gun*	गुण
queen	*rāni*	रानी
question	*prashna*	प्रश्न
quickly	*chito*	छिटो
quiet	*shānta*	शान्त
quietly	*bistārai*	बिस्तारै

R

race (sport)	*daud*	दौड
race (people)	*jāti*	जाति
racism	*jātibād*	जातिवाद
radio	*rediyo*	रेडीयो
rain (v)	*pāni parnu*	पानी पर्नु
rainy season	*barsāyām*	बर्षयाम
rare	*durlabh*	दुर्लभ
razorblade	*patti*	पत्ति
read (v)	*padhnu*	पढ्नु
ready	*tayār*	तयार
reason (n)	*kāran*	कारण
receipt	*bil*	बिल
recently	*hālsālai*	हालसालै

recommend	*siphāris garnu*	सिफारिस गर्नु
recover	*niko hunu*	निकोहुनु
refugee	*sharanārthi*	शरणार्थी
refuse (v)	*aswikār garnu*	अस्वीकार गर्नु
region	*chetra*	क्षेत्र
regulation	*niyam kānun*	नियम कानुन
relationship	*sambandha*	सम्बन्ध
relax	*ārām garnu*	आराम गर्नु
religion/philosophy	*dharma*	धर्म
remaining	*bāki*	बाकी
remember	*samjhanu*	सम्झनु
remote	*durgam*	दुर्गम
rent (n)	*bhādā*	भाडा
rent (v)	*bhādāmā linu*	भाडामा लिनु
repair (v)	*marmat garnu*	मर्मत गर्नु
representative (n)	*pratinidhi*	प्रतिनिधि
republic	*ganrājya*	गणराज्य
request (v)	*anurodh*	अनुरोध
reservation	*sancaya*	सञ्चय
reserve (v)	*sancit rākhnu*	सञ्चित राख्नु
respect (v)	*mānnu*	मान्नु
responsibility	*jimmedāri*	जिम्मेदारी
rest (v)	*ārām linu*	आराम लिनु
restaurant	*bhojanālaya*	भोजनालय
resting place (tree)	*cautārā*	चौतारा
return (v)	*pharkanu*	फर्कनु
revolution	*krānti*	क्रान्ति
rich	*dhani*	धनी
rickshaw	*rikshā*	रीक्सा

right (direction)	*dāyā̃*	दायाँ
river	*nadi*	नदि
road	*bāto*	बाटो
rock	*paharo*	पहरो
room	*kothā*	कोठा
rope	*dori*	डोरी
rough	*khasro*	खस्रो
round	*golo*	गोलो
rub (v)	*dalnu*	दल्नु
rubbish	*mailā/phohor*	मैला / फोहोर
ruins	*bhatkyo*	भत्क्यो
rupees	*rupaiyā̃*	रुपैयाँ

S

sad/sorry	*dukha*	दुःख
safe (adj)	*surachit*	सुरक्षित
safety pin	*huk*	हुक
saint	*mahātmā*	महात्मा
same	*uhi*	उही
sari	*sādi*	साडी
save	*bacāunu*	बचाउनु
say	*bhannu*	भन्नु
scared	*dar lāgdo*	डर लाग्दो
scenery	*drishya*	द्रिश्य
school	*bidyālaya*	बिद्यालय
sea	*samudra/sāgar*	समुद्र / सागर
seated (to be)	*basi rākhnu*	बसीराख्नु
secret (adj)	*gopya*	गोप्य
see/look at/watch	*hernu*	हेर्नु

see/observe	*dekhnu*	देख्नु
self	*āphu*	आफू
selfish	*swārthi*	स्वार्थी
sell	*becnu*	बेच्नु
send	*pathāunu*	पठाउनु
serious	*gambhir*	गम्भीर
servant	*nokar*	नोकर
serve	*sewā garnu*	सेवा गर्नु
shade	*shital*	शितल
shampoo	*dhulāi*	धुलाई
share (v)	*bāndnu*	बाँड्नु
shave	*khauranu*	खौरनु
shelter	*bās*	बास
shop	*pasal*	पसल
shopping	*kinmel*	किनमेल
short (height)	*pudko*	पुढ्को
(length)	*choto*	छोटो
shout (v)	*cicyāunu*	चिच्याउनु
show (v)	*dekhāunu*	देखाउनु
shower (v)	*nuhāunu*	नुहाउनु
shut	*banda garnu*	बन्द गर्नु
shyness/shame	*lāj*	लाज
sick	*birāmi*	बिरामी
side	*cheu*	छेउ
this side	*wāri*	वारि
that side	*pāri*	पारि
sign (n)	*sanket-cinha*	संङ्केत-चिन्ह
silence	*maunatā*	मौनता
silk	*resham*	रेश्म

silver	*cāndi*	चाँदि
similar	*ustai*	उस्तै
simple	*sajilo*	सजिलो
sin	*pāp*	पाप
since	*dekhi*	देखि
sing	*gāunu*	गाउनु
sitting posture	*āsana*	आसन
situation	*paristhiti*	परिस्थिति
size	*parimān*	परिमाण
sky	*ākāsh*	आकाश
sleep (n)	*nindrā*	निन्द्रा
sleep (v)	*sutnu*	सुत्नु
sleeping bag	*sutne jholā*	सुत्ने झोला
slow	*dhilo*	ढिलो
slowly	*bistārai*	बिस्तारै
small	*sāno*	सानो
small change	*khudrā paisā*	खुद्रा पैसा
smoke (v)	*(curot) khānu*	(चुरोट) खानु
snow	*hiũ*	हिउँ
soap	*sābun*	साबुन
socialism	*samājbād*	समाजवाद
sock	*mojā*	मोजा
soil	*māto*	माटो
soldier	*sipāhi*	सिपाही
solid	*thos*	ठोस
some	*kehi/kunai*	केहि / कुनै
someone	*kohi*	कोहि
something	*kehi*	केहि
sometimes	*kahile kāhĩ*	कहिलेकाहीं

son	*chorā*	छोरा
soon	*cāndai*	चाँडै
sore	*dukheko*	दुखेको
soul/spirit	*ātmā*	आत्मा
sour	*amilo*	अमिलो
south	*dachin*	दक्षिन
speak (v)	*bolnu*	बोल्नु
special	*bishes*	बिशेष
spend	*kharca garnu*	खर्च गर्नु
sport	*khelkud*	खेलकुद
spring	*basanta ritu*	बसन्त ऋतु
stamp (postage)	*hulāk tikat*	हुलाक टिकट
stand (v)	*ubhinu*	उभिनु
standard	*star*	स्तर
standing (to be)	*uthi rākhnu*	उठिराख्नु
start (v)	*suru garnu*	सुरु गर्नु
statue	*murti*	मुर्ति
stay/sit (v)	*basnu*	बस्नु
steal (v)	*cornu*	चोर्नु
steep (uphill)	*thado*	ठडो
(downhill)	*bhirālo*	भिरालो
stop (v)	*roknu*	रोक्नु
storm	*huri*	हुरी
story	*kathā*	कथा
stove (wood)	*culo*	चुलो
straight	*sidhā*	सिधा
strange	*anautho*	अनौठो
stranger	*aparicit byakti*	अपरिचित व्यक्ति

string	*dori*	डोरी
strong	*baliyo*	बलियो
student	*bidyārthi*	बिद्यार्थी
stupid	*murkha*	मूर्ख
style	*dhāncā*	धाँचा
suddenly	*acānak*	अचानक
summer	*garmi mausam*	गर्मी मौसम
sunny	*ghamāilo*	घमाईलो
sunset	*suryāsta*	सूर्यास्त
sure	*pakkā*	पक्का
surprise (n)	*chakka*	छक्क
sweet	*guliyo*	गुलियो
swim (v)	*paudi khelnu*	पौडी खेल्नु

T

table	*tebul*	टेबुल
tail	*pucchar*	पुच्छर
tailor	*sujikār*	सुजीकार
take (v)	*linu*	लिनु
talk (v)	*kurā garnu*	कुरा गर्नु
tall	*aglo*	अग्लो
telephone	*teliphon*	टेलिफोन
telephone (v)	*phon garnu*	फोन गर्नु
tell	*bhannu*	भन्नु
temperature	*tāpkram*	तापक्रम
temple (Hindu)	*mandir*	मन्दिर
(Buddhist)	*stupā*	स्तुपा

temporary	*asthāyi*	अस्थायी
tent	*pāl*	पाल
Thank you.	*dhanyabād*	धन्यवाद
that	*tyo*	त्यो
there	*tyahā̃*	त्यहाँ
these	*yi*	यि
thick	*bāklo*	बाक्लो
thief	*cor*	चोर
thin (person)	*dublo*	दुब्लो
(object)	*pātalo*	पातलो
thing (material)	*cij*	चीज
(abstract)	*kurā*	कुरा
think	*bicār garnu*	बिचार गर्नु
thirst	*tirkhā*	तिर्खा
this	*yo*	यो
those	*ti*	ति
thunder	*garjan*	गर्जन
ticket	*tikat*	टिकट
tighten (v)	*kasinu*	कस्नु
time	*samay/patak*	समय / पटक
What's the time?	*kati bajyo?*	कति बज्यो ?
timetable	*samaya tālikā*	समय तालिका
tip	*bakas*	बकस
tired	*thakāi*	थकाई
to	*-mā/-lāi*	–मा / –लाई
tobacco	*surti*	सुर्ती
today	*āja*	आज
together	*sang-sangai*	सँग-सँगै

toilet (pit)	*carpi*	चर्पि
(public)	*shaucālaya/* *pāikhānā*	शौचालय / पाईखाना
tomorrow	*bholi*	भोलि
tonight	*āja rāti*	आज राती
too	*dherai*	धेरै
total	*jammā*	जम्मा
touch (v)	*chunu*	छुनु
tour/walk (v)	*ghumnu*	घुम्नु
tourism office	*paryatan kāryālaya*	पर्यटन कार्यालय
tourist	*paryatak*	पर्यटक
towards	*tira*	तिर
towel	*rumāl*	रुमाल
town	*nagar*	नगर
trader	*sāhu*	साहु
trail	*sāno bāto*	सानो बाटो
translate	*ulthā garnu*	उल्था गर्नु
travel	*yātrā garnu*	यात्रा गर्नु
traveller	*batuwā*	बटुवा
trekking	*paidal yātrā*	पैदल यात्रा
true	*satya*	सत्य
trust (v)	*bishwās garnu*	बिश्वास गर्नु
try (v)	*kosis garnu*	कोसिस गर्नु
type	*kisim*	किसिम

U

| uncomfortable | *asajilo* | असजिलो |
| under | *muni* | मुनि |

understand	*bujhnu*	बुझ्नु
university	*bishwa bidyālaya*	बिश्वेबिद्यालय
until/up to	*samma*	सम्म
up	*māthi*	माथि
up there	*u māthi*	उ माथि
uphill	*ukālo*	उकालो
upward	*māstira*	मास्तीर
urgent/necessary	*jaruri*	जरुरी
urinate (v)	*pisāb garnu*	पिसाब गर्नु
useful	*kām lāgne*	कामलाग्ने
useless	*binākāmko*	बिनाकामको
usually	*aksar*	अक्सर
utensils	*bhā̃dākū̃dā*	भाँडाकुँडा

V

valley	*upatyakā*	उपत्यका
valuable	*bahumulya*	बहुमूल्य
vehicle	*gādi*	गाडी
very	*dherai/ekdam*	धेरै / एकदम
view	*drishya*	द्रिश्य
village	*gāũ*	गाउँ
visa	*bhisā*	भिसा
visit (v)	*bhetna jānu*	भेट्न जानु
vitamin	*bhitāmin*	भिटामिन
voice	*swar*	स्वर
vote (v)	*mat khasālnu*	मत खसाल्नु

VOCABULARY

W

wait	*parkhanu*	पर्खनु
walk (v)	*hĩḍnu*	हिंड्नु
want (v)	*cāhanu*	चाहनु
I want ...	*malāi ... cāhiyo*	मलाई ... चाहियो
war	*laḍāĩ*	लडाईं
warm	*nyāno*	न्यानो
wash (people)	*nuhāunu*	नुहाउनु
(things)	*dhunu*	धुनु
watch	*ghaḍi*	घडी
water	*pāni*	पानी
water (boiled)	*umāleko pāni*	उमालेको पानी
way	*bāto*	बाटो
Which way?	*kun bāto?*	कुन बाटो ?
we	*hāmi(haru)*	हामि(हरु)
weak	*kamjor*	कमजोर
weather	*mausam*	मौसम
wedding	*bibāha*	बिबाह
week	*haptā*	हप्ता
well	*sanco*	सन्चो
west	*pashcim*	परिचम
Westerner	*kuire*	कुइरे
wet	*bhijeko*	भिजेको
what	*ke*	के
when	*kahile*	कहिले
where	*kahā̃*	कहाँ
which	*kun*	कुन
who	*ko*	को

whole	*jammai*	जम्मै
why	*kina*	किन
wide	*pharākilo*	फराकिलो
window	*jhyāl*	झ्याल
windy	*hāwā lāgne*	हावा लाग्ने
winter	*jāḍo mahinā*	जाडो महिना
wise	*buddhimān*	बुद्धिमान
with	*-sanga/-sita/-le*	–सँग / –सित / –ले
without	*binā*	बिना
woman	*āimāi*	आइमाई
wood	*kāth*	काठ
wool	*un*	ऊन
work (n)	*kām*	काम
world	*samsār*	संसार
worried	*pir*	पिर
worse	*jhan narāmro*	झन नराम्रो
worship	*pujā*	पूजा
write (v)	*lekhnu*	लेख्नु
wrong	*bethik/galat*	बेठीक / गलत

Y

yak	*caūrigāi*	चौरीगाई
year	*barsa/sāl*	बष / साल
Yes.	*cha/ho/huncha*	छ / हो / हुन्छ
yesterday	*hijo*	हिजो
yoga	*yog*	योग
young	*jawān*	जवान
Yuck!	*chi chi*	छि छि !

Z

zone	*ancal*	अञ्चल
zoo	*cidiyā khānā*	चिडियाखाना

Emergencies

Help!	*guhār!*	गुहार !
Thief!	*cor!*	चोर !
Watch out!	*hera!*	हेर !
Go away!	*jāu!*	जाउ !

I'm lost.
   ma harāyē   म हरायें
I've been robbed.
   *corle malāi lut*yo   चोरले मलाई लुट्यो
I've been raped.
   malāi balātkār garyo   मलाई बलात्कार गर्यो

I've lost my ...	*mero ... harāyo*	मेरो ... हरायो
bag/backpack	*jholā*	झोला
camera	*kyāmerā*	क्यामेरा
money	*paisā*	पैसा
passport	*rāhadāni*	राहदानी

It's an emergency!
   āpat paryo!   आपटपर्यो !
There's been an accident!
   durghatanā bhayo!   दुर्घटना भयो !
I'm ill.
   ma birāmi chu   म बिरामी छु
Please call a doctor.
   dāktarlāi bolāunuhos   डाक्टरलाई बोलाउनुहोस

Could you help me?
*malāi maddat garna
saknu huncha?*

मलाई मद्दत गर्न सक्नुहुन्छ ?

I need to go to ...
ma ... mā jānuparcha

म ...मा जानुपर्छ

Where is the (public) toilet?
shaucālaya kahā̃ cha?

शौचालय कहाँ छ ?

I'm sorry/I apologise/
forgive me.
malāi māph garnuhos

मलाई माफ गर्नुहोस

I didn't realise I was doing
anything wrong.
*malāi thāhā bhayana
galti bhayo*

मलाई थाहा भयन गल्ती भयो

I didn't do it.
maile garinā

मैले गरिनं

Could I use the telephone?
ma teliphon garna sakincha?

म टेलिफोन गर्न सकिन्छ ?

I need to contact my embassy/
consulate.
*ma rājdutāvāsmā samparka
garnu parcha*

म राजदूतावासमा सम्पर्क
गर्नुपर्छ

Index

Abbreviations.........................9
Accommodation..................69
   Checking In.......................70
   Checking Out 75
   Complaints 74
   Finding 70
   Requests 72
Addressing People 39
Adjectives 18
Age....................................49
Ailments...........................131
Allergies...........................133
Alphabet (Nepali)........8, 11
Amounts...........................156
Animals..............................96
Asking Directions..............89
Aspirated Consonants 13
Attracting Someone's
   Attention..........................38

Bank, at the 82
Bargaining 117
Be (verb)...........................27
Bicycle Hire.......................65
Birds..................................97
Body Language 40
Body, parts of..................134
Books...............................122
Bread...............................110
Bus....................................65
Buying Tickets 64

Calendar..........................140
Camping............................99
Cardinal Numbers............156

Cereals............................109
cha 27, 30, 32, 44
Chemist............................136
Civilities.............................37
Clothing............................119
Colours............................121
Common Expressions...........42
Comparing 18
Complaints 130
Conjunctions 35
Consonants 12
Continuous Tense 24
Counters 157
Countries..........................47

Dairy Products 108
Days of the Week.............140
Dates................................141
Demonstratives 17
Devanagari script 8
Directions 62
   Asking Directions 61, 89
Doctor, at the...................129
Drinks...............................112

Embassy, at the 79
Emergencies 199
Etiquette....................40, 103

Family 51
Feelings.............................54
Festivals...........................144
Finding Your Way 61
Food.................................102
Fractions 158

Fruit 108
Future Tense..........................26
Future (time) 142

Geographical Terms 95
Getting Around......................61
Getting Started 9
Gift-Giving.............................41
Gods & Prominent Beings ...147
Grammar................................16
Greetings 37

hajur...................................38
Health 129
Herbs, Spices & Other
    Condiments.......................110
Hiring
    Bicycles 65
    Porters...............................88
ho.........................27, 28, 30
Hotel, at the 69
    Checking In 70
    Checking Out 75
    Complaints 74
    Laundry 72
    Requests 72
huncha...................27, 29, 31

Illnesses................................131
Imperative (giving orders)......32
Infinitives...............................22
Insects..................................98
Interests................................57
Interjections 59
Interrogatives........................33
Introduction............................7

Jobs 49

Kinship Terms 51

Language Difficulties.............. 44
Laundry 72
Legumes 109

Making Conversation 56
Market, at the...................... 106
    Bread..............................110
    Cereals & Legumes 109
    Dairy Products 108
    Fruit................................108
    Meat................................106
    Nuts................................110
    Vegetables 107
Materials 120
Meals 102
Measures 124
Meat 106
Medicines 129
Meeting People 46
Money 82, 115
Months (Nepali Calendar) ... 140

Nasal Vowels 11
Nationalities 47
Necessity (must) 32
Negation................................ 23
Nepali Calendar 140
Neutral Infinitive 26
No 23, 44
Nouns.................................... 17
Numbers
    Cardinal 156
    Ordinal 157
Nuts......................................110

Object Pronouns 20
Occupations 49
Opinions 56
Ordinal Numers.................... 157
'Other' 36

Parts of the Body 134
Past Tense...........................25
Past (time) 142
Pharmacy 136
Photography 83, 123
Plants..................................100
Please.................................38
Plurals.................................17
Porters, hiring 88
Possession 32
Possessive Pronouns...........21
Post Office, at the 80
Postpositions 34
Present Tense......................22
Present (time) 141
Problems
    Accommodation 74
    Health............................129
    Language 44
Professions..........................49
Pronouns 18
Pronunciation.......................11
Publications 122

Questions (making) 33

Religion................................51
Requests 32
    At the Hotel...................72
Restaurant, at the 104
Retroflex Consonants 13
Rickshaw 66

Shopping 115
Sightseeing..........................83
Size & Quantity....................124
Small Talk.............................43
Smoking................................123
Souvenirs.............................118

Special Occasions 58
Stationery 122
Stress (word) 14
Subject Pronouns................. 19

Table Articles....................... 105
Taxi...................................... 66
Telephone 81
Thank you 38
Tickets (buying).................... 64
Time 139
Tipping 41
To Be 27
Toiletries 122
Top 10 Useful Phrases......... 43
Town, around 79
Transport.............................. 63
Trekking 87
    Along the Way 91
    Directions, asking 89
    Geographical Terms....... 95
    Porters, hiring 88
    Weather 93

Vegetables 107
Vegetarian 105
Verbs.................................... 22
Vocabulary 159
Vowels.................................. 11

Water.................................... 129
Weather................................ 93
Weights................................. 124
Women's Health................... 133
Word Order 16
Word Stress 14
Work..................................... 49

Yes 44

LONELY PLANET PHRASEBOOKS

Complete your travel experience with a Lonely Planet phrasebook. Developed for the independent traveller, the phrasebooks enable you to communicate confidently in any practical situation – and get to know the local people and their culture.

Skipping lengthy details on where to get your drycleaning ironed, information in the phrasebooks covers bargaining, customs and protocol, how to address people and introduce yourself, explanations of local ways of telling the time, dealing with bureaucracy and bargaining, plus plenty of ways to share your interests and learn from locals.

Arabic (Egyptian)
Arabic (Moroccan)
Australian
   Introduction to Australian English,
   Aboriginal and Torres Strait languages.
Baltic States
   Covers Estonian, Latvian and
   Lithuanian.
Bengali
Brazilian
Burmese
Cantonese
Central Europe
   Covers Czech, French, German,
   Hungarian, Italian and Slovak.
Eastern Europe
   Covers Bulgarian, Czech, Hungarian,
   Polish, Romanian and Slovak.
Ethiopian (Amharic)
Fijian
Greek
Hindi/Urdu
Indonesian
Japanese
Korean
Lao
Latin American (Spanish)
Mandarin

Mediterranean Europe
   Covers Albanian, Greek, Italian,
   Macedonian, Maltese, Serbian &
   Croatian and Slovene.
Mongolian
Nepali
Papua New Guinea (Pidgin)
Pilipino
Quechua
Russian
Scandinavian Europe
   Covers Danish, Finnish, Icelandic,
   Norwegian and Swedish.
Sri Lanka
Swahili
Thai
Thai Hill Tribes
Tibetan
Turkish
USA
   Introduction to US English,
   Vernacular Talk, Native American
   languages and Hawaiian.
Vietnamese
Western Europe
   Useful words and phrases in Basque,
   Catalan, Dutch, French, German, Irish,
   Portuguese and Spanish (Castilian).

LONELY PLANET AUDIO PACKS

Audio packs are an innovative combination of a cassette/CD and phrasebook presented in an attractive cloth wallet made from indigenous textiles by local communities.

The cassette/CD presents each language in an interactive format. A number of successful language teaching techniques are used, enabling listeners to remember useful words and phrases with little effort and in an enjoyable way.

Travellers will learn essential words and phrases – and their correct pronunciation – by participating in a realistic story. The scripts have been developed in the belief that the best way to learn a new language is to hear it, then to practise it in the context in which you will use it. The emphasis is on effective communication.

The cassette/CD complements the relevant phrasebook, and the cloth wallet makes the pack an attractive and convenient package – easy to display in shops and useful and practical for travellers.

Cassettes & CDs
- complement phrasebooks
- realistic storylines explore situations that will be useful for all travellers
- languages are spoken by native speakers
- listeners learn key words and phrases in repetition exercises, then hear them used in context
- realistic sound effects and indigenous music used throughout
- length: 80 minutes

Cloth Pack
- ticket-wallet size – suitable for airline tickets, notes etc
- made from traditional textiles woven and sewn by local communities
- cardboard reinforced and sealed in plastic for easy display
- size: 140 x 260 mm

Available now: Indonesian audio pack; Japanese audio pack; Thai audio pack

PLANET TALK

Lonely Planet's FREE quarterly newsletter

Every issue is packed with up-to-date travel news and advice including:

- a letter from Lonely Planet co-founders Tony and Maureen Wheeler
- go behind the scenes on the road with a Lonely Planet author
- feature article on an important and topical travel issue
- a selection of recent letters from travellers
- details on forthcoming Lonely planet promotions
- complete list of Lonely Planet products

To join our mailing list contact any Lonely Planet office.

LONELY PLANET PUBLICATIONS

AUSTRALIA
PO Box 617, Hawthorn 3122, Victoria
tel: (03) 9819 1877 fax: (03) 9819 6459
e-mail: talk2us@lonelyplanet.com.au

USA
Embarcadero West,
155 Filbert St, Suite 251,
Oakland, CA 94607
tel: (510) 893 8555
TOLL FREE: 800 275-8555
fax: (510) 893 8563
e-mail: info@lonelyplanet.com

UK
10 Barley Mow Passage, Chiswick,
London W4 4PH
tel: (0181) 742 3161 fax: (0181) 742 2772
e-mail: 100413.3551@compuserve.com

FRANCE:
71 bis rue du Cardinal Lemoine, 75005
Paris
tel: 1 44 32 06 20 fax: 1 46 34 72 55
e-mail: 100560.415@compuserve.com

World Wide Web: http://www.lonelyplanet.com